# THE FOUNDER'S MANUAL

# The Founder's Manual

A
**Guidebook**
for Becoming a
**Successful**
Entrepreneur

RYAN FREDERICK

Paramount Market Publishing, Inc.

Paramount Market Publishing, Inc.
274 North Goodman Street, STE D-214
Rochester, NY 14607
www.paramountbooks.com
607-275-8100

Publisher: James Madden
Editorial Director: Doris Walsh

Copyright © 2020 Ryan Frederick
First published USA 2020
Printed in USA

All rights reserved. No part of this book may be reproduced, stored in a retrieval system, or transmitted in any form or by any means, electronic, mechanical, photocopying, recording, or otherwise, without the prior written permission of the publisher. Further information may be obtained from Paramount Market Publishing, Inc., 274 North Goodman Street, STE D-214, Rochester, NY 14607.

Cataloging in Publication Data available
ISBN-10: 1-941688-68-3
ISBN-13: 978-1-941688-68-7
eISBN: 978-1-941688-69-4

# Contents

| | |
|---|---|
| Foreword | vii |
| **Founder Flow** | **1** |
|     Chapter 1  Introduction | 3 |
|     Chapter 2  Self-awareness | 5 |
|     Chapter 3  Risk | 25 |
|     Chapter 4  Discipline | 28 |
|     Chapter 5  First, Best | 36 |
|     Chapter 6  Be a Great Storyteller | 39 |
|     Chapter 7  The Rest of Your Life | 43 |
|     Chapter 8  Convicted Flexibility | 53 |
|     Chapter 9  Emotional Quotient (EQ) | 58 |
|     Chapter 10 Recruiting | 62 |
|     Chapter 11 Ego | 65 |
|     Chapter 12 Long Game, Immediate Focus | 71 |
|     Chapter 13 Introverts | 76 |
|     Chapter 14 Order | 80 |
|     Chapter 15 Run to the Fire | 87 |
| **Startup Flow** | **95** |
|     Chapter 16 Introduction | 97 |
|     Chapter 17 Niche First | 99 |
|     Chapter 18 Manage to Pro Forma | 101 |
|     Chapter 19 Fail Fast is BS | 104 |
|     Chapter 20 Service to Product | 106 |
|     Chapter 21 Be Investable | 109 |

| | |
|---|---|
| Chapter 22 Timing | 114 |
| Chapter 23 Constraints | 117 |
| Chapter 24 Product Management | 122 |
| Chapter 25 Accelerators | 127 |
| Chapter 26 Sales | 133 |
| Chapter 27 Fund Through Customers | 137 |
| Chapter 28 Culture and Branding | 142 |
| **Product Flow** | **147** |
| Chapter 29 Introduction | 149 |
| Chapter 30 Roadmap (and an Agile rant) | 151 |
| Chapter 31 Hypothesis | 154 |
| Chapter 32 Feature Seeking | 156 |
| Chapter 33 Speed Matters | 159 |
| Chapter 34 Get and Stay Close to Customers | 162 |
| Chapter 35 Outcomes Over Outputs | 167 |
| Chapter 36 Ship Early and Often | 169 |
| Chapter 37 Small, Committed, Skilled Team | 171 |
| Chapter 38 Don't Find a Solution Too Early | 174 |
| Chapter 39 Pay Little (no) Attention to Competitors | 177 |
| Chapter 40 Don't be the X of Y | 181 |
| Chapter 41 The Best, Not First, Product Wins | 184 |
| Final Thoughts | 187 |
| Acknowledgments | 189 |
| About the Author | 193 |

# Foreword

I'm a product person and Founder at heart. I've been part of building too many software products to count, privileged to be part of starting and growing six software companies, and am now a Principal in an elite product and data consulting firm and an angel investor. Over time I have mentored and advised dozens of Founders, startups, and product people. I speak regularly on creating products and building companies. I wrote this book because I became intrigued by Flow several years ago and began asking if Flow could be achieved in building products, being a Founder, and starting companies.

Flow is a state most often associated with athletes performing at a high level, seemingly without trying. This state is often characterized as being "in the zone." Mihály Csíkszentmihályi identified Flow as a concept in 1975 and is considered to be the first person to study it in any depth. Flow became more widely known through the research and writings of Steven Kotler in his books *Rise of Superman* and *Stealing Fire*. Steven also cofounded the Flow Genome Project with Jamie Wheal.

As I dug deeper into understanding Flow, its components, and the dynamics of how it is achieved, I kept going back to this question: "Could creating products, being a Founder and starting companies achieve Flow? Are there components to creating each situation, that if leveraged at the right time and in the right mix, could increase the chances of success? The answer became a resounding yes and this book is the result of the pursuit of an answer to that question.

I called on my own experiences creating products and being part of starting companies, those I have mentored and advised, the ones I have invested in, and the ones with which my consulting firm has engaged. A pattern of components developed that, if combined and executed properly, increased the likelihood a product, Founder, and company would be successful. It also turns out that achieving flow reduces the time and cost of creating a successful product, eases the journey of being a Founder, and makes the mercurial existence of a startup a little more predictable and manageable.

Creating anything of meaning and value is a challenging endeavor. Add doing it in a way that a commercially viable company exists to take a product to market and for both to be sustainable, yikes. It is the professional equivalent of climbing Mt. Everest. The teams that climb Mt. Everest prepare and plan, understanding and accounting for the circumstances they will certainly face, and for the ones they might face. The teams hire an experienced guide, in most cases, someone who has successfully climbed the mountain before. The guides provide an approach and expertise based on their experience and principles they know to be true about increasing the odds of successfully and safely ascending and descending the mountain. My intention in writing this book is to help you to increase the odds of success of the often treacherous path to build products or start companies. Let's begin . . .

# Founder Flow

**CHAPTER 1**

# Introduction

There isn't one way to be a successful Founder. There is no right way, but there are many wrong ways. Being a Founder is a personal and unique journey. However, there are principles that can help Founders be better and increase their odds of starting and growing a successful company.

The principles in this section to help Founders to achieve Flow include:
- Discipline
- Self-awareness
- Risk muscle
- Being a great storyteller
- First, best everything (to start)
- Convicted flexibility
- Recruiting
- Emotional Quotient (EQ)

Keep in mind as you are going through the principles that they are focused on Founders building successful companies. Through the process of building a successful company, Founders will have a lot of fun, get access to a lot of new and interesting experiences, meet many dynamic people, and evolve beyond a Founder's wildest dreams. Some of the principles don't seem all that fun; in fact, they aren't. Some of the principles are counter-intuitive. Most go against human nature. And all will challenge you, all of the time. The principles reinforce the difficulty of building a successful company. The principles, leveraged properly, will also help separate Founders—from pretenders to contenders. These principles will help a Founder who embraces them and uses them consistently to focus on the right things, with the right mindset to be the problem solver and leader they are capable of being. This is the essence of being a Founder.

*Note:* Founder is used to represent individual Founders and a group of Founders

## CHAPTER 2
# Self-awareness

Self-awareness is critical to being a successful Founder. Founders are confronted with untold and unknown circumstances. A Founder's ability to know how to react to varying situations, stresses, and pressures is critical to being successful.

## A Choice

Being a Founder is a choice. I see many Founders expecting their families, friends, former coworkers, and the world at large to honor the fact they have chosen to be a Founder. I had this mindset early on too. I wanted everyone to acknowledge how hard it is to be a Founder and that I had enough courage to be part of starting companies. It is hard of course, but no one owes you anything for choosing to be a Founder and taking the journey. You make the choice to be a Founder for yourself. Seeking recognition for doing so is a sign of doing it for the wrong reasons. I know, I've been there. Being a Founder is one way to prove to the world you are someone and that you are taking on the most challenging professional endeavor anyone can. Being a Founder to prove other people wrong, or for any other reason that is more about other people than you, is dangerous and most of the time ill-fated. Using other people's doubts and skepticism of your ability to be a successful Founder can be fuel, but it shouldn't be the reason you are starting a company. Starting a company for any reason other than to solve a high-value problem people care about is likely not to go or end well. So choose to be a Founder because you are compelled and capable of solving a problem that improves the lives or businesses of customers and not for any ego, fear, or other reason. Being a Founder doesn't make you inherently special. If you think it does, you are probably doing it for the wrong reasons and shouldn't be a Founder. If you see being a Founder as a privilege to be a problem solver that improves lives and the world in some small or maybe massive way, then you are probably choosing wisely to be one.

Being a Founder doesn't make you special, but it does make you different. This is an important distinction. Yes, choosing to be a Founder is a unique professional path and challenge that most people don't want any part of and they shouldn't. Most people are not cut out to be Founders and shouldn't do it. I believe this is like 98 percent of people, maybe more. Being a Founder goes against almost all of Maslow's Hierarchy of Needs and how we are inherently wired as people. After having experienced it myself and having a front row seat to thousands of other Founders, I'm convinced the journey is meant for a very small percentage of people. It might even be less than two percent.

This is one of the reasons the world of venture capital is more difficult than it appears on the surface. VC's are looking for the two percent. The two percent returns the entirety of their investments. Being a Venture Capitalist appears to be easy on the surface—meet with a lot of excited entrepreneurs about innovative, new products and business models and write checks. What's not to like? Investors invest in people. Yes, products and yes, markets, but it begins and ends with the team.

So the real job of investors is to determine the capability and veracity of the team—the two percent. With first time Founders the challenge is even greater because investors don't have much to go on. That's why you will often see repeat Founders, even failed ones, getting investment over first-time Founders. With repeat Founders, investors can create a profile of the Founders that increases the confidence they are in the two percent, while for first-time Founders, investors are taking much more of a flyer. This is another reason why much of Venture Capital has moved to the Series A and later rounds and less is available in the early rounds. Almost all angel, pre-seed, and seed investing is taking a gamble on whether the Founders are in the two percent. Of course as the percentages indicate, most of the time they aren't and the companies and investments go to zero.

Don't confuse being different with being special and know that being different isn't worth that much either unless you are different enough as a Founder to be in the two percent.

## Emotions

Being a Founder is a roller coaster of emotions. A Founder's awareness of his or her emotions and controlling those emotions not only helps the Founder to stay focused and to execute well, but it also instills confidence in the team, customers, investors, partners, and other stakeholders. Founders will experience the highest of highs and the lowest of lows launching and growing a company. How well a Founder deals with and manages the ups and downs dictates the culture of the company and the temperament of all involved. Founders that can achieve a balanced approach to stay as emotionally even-keeled as possible have a better and healthier existence and instill the same balanced perspective in the team. Founders need to understand what triggers emotion for them, why it's a trigger, and how they react. Founders cannot perform at an optimal level without emotional control and understanding.

## Decision Making

Founders need to be great decision makers. They need to be decisive, frequently with incomplete information. Being a great decision maker is challenging for anyone, but it is heightened for Founders. Founders need to understand how they make decisions and to establish a set of guiding principles they apply to making decisions. Principles that guide decision making can include:

- What's the impact of doing nothing?
- Who is most impacted?
- Is this in the best interest of us, the product, the company, customers?
- What are the derivative impacts of the decision?

## Loneliness

Being a Founder can be a very lonely existence. Partners, family, and friends may have a difficult time understanding and relating to what Founders experience. Founders invest so much energy dealing with the ups and downs it often leaves them with little energy left over to deal with other things and relationships. Founders need to be self-aware enough to know when they are getting drained, depressed, and lonely so they can acknowledge it and deal with it. Feelings of loneliness can turn into feelings of isolation and abandonment, which can be serious and have long lasting detrimental consequences. Feeling lonely doesn't just happen when things aren't going well with the company either. I, and many others I've known, have felt lonely and isolated when the company was doing well. The mercurial journey of being a Founder can take its toll and can change people as part of the journey—for the better and for worse. If you are a Founder now or become one and you have feelings of loneliness and despair, you need to seek professional help immediately. You are more valuable than the business will ever be.

## Imposter syndrome

Imposter syndrome is something many Founders experience. Essentially imposter syndrome is the feeling of not belonging because you haven't accomplished enough, aren't smart enough, and other "not enough." I have experienced this and I know many Founders who also have. As a Founder everyone around you seems to know what should be done and how to do it better than you. Everyone also has advice for you, mostly about what you are doing wrong or haven't done. All of these perspectives and opinions foster imposter syndrome and deepen the feelings. There is no easy fix to imposter syndrome. Every Founder has to overcome it step by step. One day and one accomplishment at a time. Relapses are common and can be frequent even when you've begun to quell the feelings. A sale doesn't happen, an important customer leaves, a valued team member moves on to something else. Any negative outcome can bring the imposter syndrome feelings back. When the feelings come back after making some progress to quell them it can feel like a flood and can take you back to your earliest, most acute imposter moments. Eventually it gets easier to bounce back and to overcome the feelings. Each occurrence strengthens your resiliency until you stop having the feelings and have demonstrated to yourself you've earned the right to be where you are and do what you're doing.

Even the most confident and experienced Founders still question themselves constantly. It gets marginally easier with every decision that goes well and it gets eroded again with every decision that doesn't turn out for the best. The pressure and spotlight of customers, the team, board members, investors, and advisors heightens the emotions and stakes.

## Not romantic

Being a Founder is really being a problem solver. When someone tells me they want to be a Founder, I ask them what problem they are solving and the typical response is, "I don't know yet. I just want to be an entrepreneur so I can be my own boss." That's not a good enough reason to be a Founder (entrepreneur). If that is your mindset, you will be the worst person you've ever worked for, you will waste a lot of time, and probably a fair amount of money. Being a Founder is not romantic, nor sexy. It is a grind in every sense of the word and experience. The one thing I know for certain about being a

Founder is that if someone calls himself or herself a Founder or entrepreneur for the sake of having that headline on their LinkedIn profile or social media accounts and they aren't actively working to solve a problem, they are playing Founder for the romance of it. Being a Founder or entrepreneur is a title anyone can give themselves, but it doesn't make you one. Jason Fried, Founder of Basecamp, recently tweeted, "Don't start an up, start a business." Yes!

## Freedom

Many people want to be a Founder because they want freedom. They want to do what they want, when they want. Although it's true that being a Founder brings a certain degree of independence and freedom, Founders still have people to answer to, including themselves. Others include customers, the team, investors, a board, and partners. Because no one is telling Founders how to spend their time and watching everything they do, new Founders can become enamored with the independence and then it can be difficult for them to turn on working hard and being disciplined when they need it. Working hard and being disciplined are not switches that can be flipped to catch-up for lost time. Time used irresponsibly can never be recovered. Freedom from someone telling you what to do is dangerous for many. The freedom is power and it has to be used wisely and responsibly. Founders seeking to "Be my own boss" who don't have anyone telling them what to do, when to do it, and how do it are destined to be disappointed when they realize they have stakeholders they are accountable to with the first and most important one being themselves (the company).

Being a successful Founder isn't about playing business, it **is** business. Everyone in business has people they serve and obligations as part of that service. Founders who view being a Founder as a get-out-of-work-free card are not yet ready to be a Founder. Be a Founder to be a successful problem solver and businessperson, period. The fringe benefits that come along the way, like having more time to schedule freedom, are derivatives of being successful.

## Comfortable with discomfort

Founders need to get comfortable being uncomfortable. Most aspects of being a Founder and starting a company are new and uncomfortable. Founders that don't get comfortable with being in a perpetual state of discomfort will struggle to be positive, resilient, and to be great leaders. I've seen many Founders struggle to be successful because of never coming to terms with the constant state of not knowing things and what problems lie around the corner for their companies. There will be constant new problems to solve and in some cases no way to predict them. That's the deal. That's what Founders sign up for. They just don't know until they are in it. This also can't be observed or explained. Watching another Founder go through it isn't the same. Having Founders tell you about their experience isn't the same. Observing and hearing about the experiences of other Founders can help and that's one of the reasons I'm involved in a global organization to help connect, educate, and inspire Founders, called Startup Grind (startupgrind.com), but to understand the experience of being a Founder you have to do it. Being a Founder is a personal journey.

There are many ways to begin to get comfortable with being uncomfortable. One way is to do things differently than most people, not for the sake of being different, but for the value it brings you. A simple one that anyone can do is to take cold showers. We take hot showers because they make us feel better and are more soothing. We are creatures of comfort and ease, which isn't always awesome for being a Founder. Cold showers are actually better for your hair and your overall health too. I started taking cold showers initially because it was better for my hair and to help my body recover from workouts. I then realized it was bringing me so much more value. First, if you live in a place that gets cold weather, taking cold showers helps you acclimate to the cold easier making it more comfortable to be outside when it's cold and when others are hibernating. Second, a cold shower is invigorating. If you typically shower first thing in the morning it will help kickstart your day. If you shower later in the day it will get you reenergized. Third, it reduces your energy consumption. Not using hot water to shower will lower your utility expense by using less electricity or gas. So if you are looking for a place to start getting comfortable with being uncomfortable, start taking cold showers.

## Situational awareness

Self-awareness helps Founders be situationally aware. Situational awareness is important for Founders because Founders are confronted with so many decisions and challenges, often at the same time. Founders need to be able to read and interpret what is happening and make decisions with the information they have, which might not be much, to keep moving quickly and making progress. It's hard to be situationally aware if you aren't self-aware because situational awareness is an extension of self-awareness. Knowing how you process information and make decisions effectively is what allows you to have good, effective situational awareness.

## Dysfunctional background

There have been several stories written about people from dysfunctional families and backgrounds making better entrepreneurs. Steve Blank, a friend and supporter of Startup Grind, has written about this a couple of times. I agree with the underlying premise, but with some qualifiers. Being from a dysfunctional background does develop a muscle for getting comfortable with being uncomfortable and creates a degree of agency. Knowing you can be confronted with unknown events and circumstances beyond your control teaches you to focus on what you can control and trains you to expect the unexpected. Experiencing a chaotic and fluid family environment and childhood can be a terrific training ground for being a Founder and entrepreneur.

***Can be*** is the operative part of the last sentence and the reason I'm referencing it as part of Founder self-awareness. Founders have to be balanced and I've seen Founders from challenging circumstances that carry positives out of it, but also many that carry negatives out of it that outweigh and dominate the positives. Founders who come from challenging circumstances can be defensive, protective, and combative. It often manifests with the Founders being distrustful and being defiant with people who are genuinely trying to help them. It can be difficult for Founders from dysfunctional backgrounds to understand why someone would want to help them. These Founders can sometimes embrace competitors and known enemies more readily than people who are trying to help them. The competitors and enemies have identified themselves and chosen a side. That's easy for Founders to understand and deal with. But experience also tells them that many people in their lives have come and gone only to take advantage of the Founders when these people initially seemed well intentioned, ultimately to leave the Founder bruised, jaded, and weary. Founders from dysfunctional backgrounds should not blindly trust people, as this can be a recipe for more of the same of what they've already experienced. However, these Founders eventually need to trust and depend on people who are trustworthy and dependable. The trust and dependability is earned, not given. But when someone earns it through demonstrated action, Founders need to be able to appreciate it, value it, and embrace it. Founders from dysfunctional backgrounds who continue to fight circumstances of the past now and in the future will remain in the past and will let those circumstances be an anchor to their development and progress which will inevitably affect that of the company.

None of the above is to say you can't be a successful Founder from a positive, nourishing, and stable background. Of course you can. What some of Steve Blank's articles point out around the dysfunctional backgrounds that can be good for Founders can be bad for Founders that come from stable backgrounds. If a Founder's family and broader environment was very stable and without a lot of tumult, the Founder may not be prepared and may not have the coping skills to deal with any, let alone a lot, of chaos and fluidity. I've seen Founders with an abundance of support, resources, and stability in their lives who don't succeed because they couldn't deal with the roller coaster ride that comes along with being a Founder. My advice for Founders that are from a background heaped with stability and certainty is to put themselves in situations that aren't, often with increasing challenge and uncertainty. Founders who have never had to deal with chaos will be unprepared to deal with it when it arises, which is constantly in a startup.

## Underestimated

Founders are my people and tribe. Underestimated Founders in particular. I grew up in a small town in Upstate New York. My parents were lower-middle income. No entrepreneurial fabric in my family. I was an average student and dropped out of technical school (I did get a business degree later in life). Not exactly the formula for someone to have entrepreneurial thoughts and desires; so I get underestimated Founders. It would be taking it too far to say I can relate to all underestimated Founders. I can't. I'm white and a male. I will never know the experiences and challenges of being another race or gender. But I do get being underestimated. It's one of the reasons I helped to launch an organization called BLK hack which is working to plug more black people into the startup and venture ecosystems. BLK hack is about to launch a Venture Combine in Columbus to help more underestimated people understand how venture works and how to leverage it. I'm also part of a group preparing to launch a

Women's Venture Studio so we can help more women launch and grow companies, including helping them secure funding from female investors by getting more high-net-worth women to become angel investors. We're just getting started on this, but we're optimistic that we can make an impact on the number of women starting high-growth companies and receiving a larger share of venture investment. The stats on the percent of venture investment that goes to female Founders is embarrassingly low and increasing too slowly. We aim to facilitate more venture investment and support for female Founders.

Underestimated Founders do have it harder than those Founders who aren't. It's the reality. It doesn't make it right, but coming to terms with it and dealing with the reality is better than pretending it isn't different. I'm not saying to give in or give up, I'm saying the opposite. Understand it. Don't get caught up in bemoaning it. Work your ass off and go from being underestimated to undeniable. If you are an underestimated Founder use it to your advantage. Yes, you will have to do everything 10 times better than other Founders. Get over it. Do it. Be present. Be visible. Be 10 times better and undeniable to customers, investors, and partners. Intent and discipline matter even more for underestimated Founders. Intent and discipline have no biases. They just call you to do what needs to be done right now. And to not stop until you've accomplished what you set out to do. The world honors and respects relentless, consistent discipline and execution irrespective of who is doing it, what they look like, and what their background is. If you want to go from underestimated to undeniable, execute with relentless, unending discipline.

Being an underestimated Founder doesn't mean you deserve anything. I meet underestimated Founders who have the perspective of being deserving of help, support, and success. I've been there. When you see other people who come from backgrounds of more means, more support, and more connections, it's easy to fall into the trap of feeling you got gipped because of the hand you were dealt. The cold, harsh reality is no one cares. And you shouldn't either. You can't change the circumstance of the hand you were dealt and the circumstances you were born into. You can change your attitude around it and not give into it. If you have a deserving mindset currently, change it to an earning mindset. Meaning you don't deserve anything; none of us do, but you can earn whatever you want. Use being underestimated to your advantage. Let it drive you and be your fuel to be 10 times better.

When underestimated Founders break out, the world needs to watch out. Underestimated Founders have pent up energy and intent that serves as fuel for when they find the right thing to apply it to. Underestimated Founder's worlds often start out small and can remain small for a fairly long period of time in some cases. They have a sense there is more to the world and their place in it, than they directly know and can describe. Underestimated Founders typically don't come from entrepreneurial families and circumstances either, which makes them call into question their entrepreneurial ambitions until they realize they can't shake the desire to solve problems and create things. When the ambition finds a problem to solve and the world begins to open up for underestimated Founders they become a force to be reckoned with. Underestimated Founders stepping into the bigger world they had an inkling existed when their world was small is one of the most glorious things to witness. I've lived this. As I mentioned earlier, I grew up in a small town in Upstate New York, the son of lower-middle income parents. It was in many ways a typical, rural upbringing. I was also extremely shy. I didn't begin to break out of the shyness until I was 18 and moved away from home. The combination of where I grew up and being extremely shy meant my world was really small. I got glimpses of the world being bigger and somehow began to understand that although my world was small, I was getting an occasional peek into an existence that was much grander, endlessly challenging, and interesting in so many ways. This glimpse came mostly through sports. I've always enjoyed sports and recall seeing games played in far off, exotic locales like Los Angeles, San Diego, and Miami. I wondered what it was like to live in places like that and also began to realize that everyone who owned sports teams owned their own companies. I think that is when I started to get the entrepreneurial bug and began thinking about starting and owning my own companies. My parents were not entrepreneurial; I had some distant relatives who were, but did not see them very often and didn't know them well. So where does the entrepreneurial desire come from for people who come from small worlds and no close entrepreneurial exposure? I don't know. I've been asking myself that my entire adult life and still don't have the answer. What I do know is that once you start thinking about it and develop the desire to be a Founder, it never goes away. It becomes something you are compelled to act on. It becomes something you have to challenge yourself with and once you know you want to be a Founder it is a potential you have to fulfill.

## Slow things down

Founders need to find ways to slow things down for themselves while the product and company are and should be moving really fast. A Founder's ability to slow themselves down has a direct correlation to the product and company being able to move fast. I know, it doesn't make sense on the surface, but it's true. A Founder who is frantic, scrambling, and thrashing about is a detriment to the product and company. A Founder running around almost always means the product and company aren't. The Founder is absorbing and consuming a lot of the team's and company's energy in support of the Founder's own pace. The Founder in this case sucks energy out of the company instead of putting it in.

There are many ways for Founders to slow down. Meditation, doing yoga, reading, painting, writing, and experiencing nature are a few. A Founder has to find the medium that makes the most sense and works best for them to be still and quiet their mind and body. The purpose of slowing down is to do just that, quiet the mind and body. A Founder's ability to quiet themselves gives them more clarity and control when confronted with difficult and often unexpected problems and decisions. Founders who can quiet their minds while making decisions make better, more-reasoned decisions than those who can't. Quiet elicits composure. Founders who are composed engender confidence in the team, customers, investors, and partners. Composure comes to some Founders naturally, but typically it is developed over time through experience and being grounded in an intentional effort to be more composed through times of practiced quiet.

Developing the ability to be quiet doesn't always come easily and for many Founders it is a significant challenge, because Founders are wired to do and act. If you are struggling with quieting yourself and things like meditation aren't working initially, simplify it. Being quiet is a very personal and individual thing. One thing to try first if you are struggling is to limit your noise factor and inputs. While getting around, don't listen to any music, podcasts, or news. Just listen and be. If you listen to things while exercising or going for a walk, don't. Just listen and be. A key aspect of being quiet and achieving internal quiet is to limit your inputs. Limit and filter your inputs with unparalleled rigor. Be ultra-selective on what you listen to, read, and watch. A constant stream of anything won't allow you to learn to be quiet and to reap the benefits. This is true even with presumably valuable content. There are many terrific podcasts, blogs, audio books, and newsletters across the spectrum of being a Founder and start-ups. Consume them in reasonable and managed portions, allowing for quiet time for you to internalize and reflect on what you've heard, read, and learned.

Being quiet and getting the benefits out of it doesn't mean you have to become a world-class stoic, it simply means you have to find ways that work for you to slow down your thoughts and reactions to things so you can operate at a higher-level and with more control.

## You 2.0

Being a Founder will challenge and change you. It will

amplify your strengths and weaknesses personally and professionally. If you take a serious run at starting and growing a company you will be changed and different from the person you were before. Sometimes for the better and sometimes for the worse, but you will be changed. People close to you will notice and will comment on it. These are sometimes complimentary perspectives like: "I've never seen you more focused," "more disciplined," "more determined," "happier," or "fulfilled." But they can also be derogatory perspectives like; "you're not as much fun," "all you want to talk about is the company," "you're boring," "you're selfish." The selfish one is my favorite and I now know to actually spin that as a positive remark because if you are being intentional and disciplined it will come across to some people as being selfish. That's okay. I saw a Tweet recently from Justin Kan (Justin is an entrepreneur and investor) that said, "You can have anything you want, but you can't have everything you want." I wholeheartedly agree. This is a fundamental tenant of being intentional and disciplined. You have to choose what you want and what price you are willing to pay to obtain it. Paying a price also means what are you going to give up. Note the wording of the previous sentence—what you are going to give up, means actually giving things up. I often see it worded and hear people say, "willing to give up." Being willing to give something up isn't the same as actually giving it up. Willing is theoretical. Giving is doing it.

    The good news is you get to control how being a Founder changes you. You can use the challenges of being a Founder to improve and evolve or to succumb and devolve. I've experienced both and I've witnessed both. You might have to get knocked down and be bruised before and until you are ready to be changed for the better and to leverage the journey to evolve personally and professionally. Part of this process and evolution is to be honest with yourself. Admit when you mess up and don't handle something as you should. None of us are at our best all the time. This percentage goes down for Founders as we are challenged to be at our best all the time and when we fall short we internalize and take it personally. Do that, but ask yourself how you could have done better and handled the situation better. Was it a lack of understanding, knowledge, or skill that can be improved upon? Was it a lack of personal emotional control? How can you identify when it is happening and prevent it from happening in the future or at least diminish the impact and lessen the consequences? You also get to celebrate and acknowledge your evolution as it is happening and there is no other professional endeavor that provides the same trajectory for evolution that being a Founder does. You will understand not only yourself better, but other people as well. You will get a crash course in business that no MBA course can come close to delivering. The highs and lows will be extreme and part of your growth is to navigate it all with a controlled responsibility that, when done well, is a sight to behold.

## Be You

Throughout the journey and all of the personal evolution and change, every Founder needs to be theirself. Founders can't and shouldn't try to be someone else. They shouldn't try to emulate other Founders. Unless a Founder knows other Founders personally they don't know the flaws of any other

Founders. Emulating even what appears to be a successful Founder is the wrong approach for any new Founder. Understanding and following principles, such as the ones I've laid out in this book, provides Founders with a good foundation to work from and allows Founders to be themselves on top of the principles. Investors, advisors, and countless others will offer advice and might even suggest that a Founder study and act like other Founders. I'm all for studying successful people, but unless you get a chance to know someone beyond the surface and outward appearances you don't really know them. New Founders establishing relationships with other more experienced, successful Founders can be valuable as long as the new Founder is comfortable with who they are and is learning new ways of approaching running their own company, and not taking on a me-too perspective. You are enough. The evolving, growing, improving you is getting better with every passing moment if you understand and act on principles of being a successful Founder.

If you've already started a company and aren't as self-aware as you need to be, begin to take steps to do so, right now. If you aren't a Founder yet, take the steps to be self-aware before you become one. A Founder's ability to lead others and to succeed is in direct relation to the Founder's ability to understand, direct, and lead themselves. Founders should not expect to be able to understand, coach, and lead others if they can't do it with themselves.

## CHAPTER 3
# Risk

Most people avoid risk. Some avoid it at all costs. I'm talking about real risk. Real risk has physical, mental, emotional, or financial harm at stake. This is one of things that makes Founders unique. Embracing and even running toward risk is an unusual human action.

We're not wired to embrace risk. In fact, we are wired to avoid risk. Risk avoidance is reinforced as we grow up. Parents tell their kids not to climb too high in a tree or not to climb at all. Founders are told they are crazy and are asked why they can't hold a job like normal people. Outdoor adventurists are often labeled as trouble makers or counter culture. The list goes on. Risks have consequences. Because negative consequences are often the primary focus of taking chances, we avoid risk and any associated danger or harm.

The problem with risk avoidance is that nothing changes, advances, gets discovered, or solved without someone taking a risk—and potentially risking everything. Embracing risk and getting good at managing and leveraging it are skills everyone who wants to affect change needs to develop. It can be done. The most successful Founders develop a positive relationship with risk.

Strengthening your risk muscle begins with taking small

risks with limited negative consequences and escalating the level of risk over time. The frequency of engaging with risk is also important. If you go too long between engaging with and experiencing risk, you won't develop any risk muscle memory. Each new risk experience will be starting from scratch and you won't evolve mentally, emotionally, or physically. Your self-awareness around engaging with risk is paramount to getting better at it. You need to be mindful of and track how you feel, what you are thinking, and how your body is reacting when you engage in any risky situations. As you engage with risk, you will get better at assessing risk based on your capabilities and confidence.

As your risk muscle strengthens, you also need to decide what aspects of life you are comfortable taking risks in, but be mindful not to allow risk avoidance in one area of life to weaken your risk muscle in other areas.

## Get Physical First

All types of risks have mental, emotional, and physical impacts. Go rock climbing or do any other potentially risky physical activity and see how your mind and emotions react in addition to the physical ones. Physical risks are a good place to start and build upon. Physical risks have mental and emotional risks associated to them in addition to what might happen physically. Physical risks require mental and emotional focus to overcome the challenge, so they test more than just your physical limits. The physical risks I'm speaking about need to have the real potential for physical harm to be effective in strengthening your risk muscle. There have to be negative consequences associated to any activity to make it a risk and for your risk muscle to strengthen.

## Emotional Risk

Emotional risk might be the hardest one to overcome. About 75 percent of people have a fear of public speaking, according to various studies. The fear of public speaking is rooted in emotional risk and ego protection. No one wants to look or sound stupid and be embarrassed. This feeling is so powerful that really smart, capable people avoid public speaking at all costs. As with physical risks, emotional risks have mental and physical aspects. If you get into an uncomfortable emotional situation you perceive as risky, how does your body react? Does your heart beat faster? Do you sweat? Do you start talking slower or faster than normal?

## Financial Risk

Financial risks are really emotional at their core. I'm breaking it out separately from emotional risks because many people see financial risks differently than emotional ones. More money can be made if you lose it. Our concern for financial loss is almost always about ego and how other people will view our success or lack thereof if we lose financially.

You can strengthen your risk muscle over time by:
- Taking incrementally more challenging risks across the spectrum of physical, emotional, and financial areas.
- Doing so at a consistent pace.
- Tracking how you feel, how you performed, and where you still need to improve.

Doing this will help you get good at assessing risks based on your current risk-muscle evolution.

## CHAPTER 4

# Discipline

Intention and discipline trump everything else. Intention and discipline are undeniable. The universe takes note of discipline and honors it. So do a team, customers, investors, partners, and well, everyone that matters to a Founder. Founders who are disciplined have a chance to do and build something incredible. Founders who aren't, don't. It's that simple. Starting and growing a company is too hard and too fragile to do without intense discipline.

It seems we have entered an era in which being a Founder and entrepreneur has become romantic and sexy. As a result, I see too many Founders who appear to be more interested in being a celebrity (mostly in their local startup community) than actually operating and succeeding with the company. It has never been easier to start a business and it's never been harder to build a successful one. Founders, don't get lured by grabbing a mic every chance you get. And if you are grabbing a mic, know why you are doing it and what outcome you expect to get out of it. You might speak for recruiting the team, acquiring customers, establishing partnerships, or visibility with investors. Just don't speak to massage your own ego. Inflating your ego does nothing to help the company progress and execute.

Hustle is on fire. It's everywhere. And it seems to represent a new perspective on how to be successful at almost an epiphany level. I hope we've reached peak Hustle because it sends the wrong message.

I see a lot people, startup Founders and beyond, wearing Hustle as a badge of honor. You should be hustling to accomplish what you want. Hustle is not a destination. Additionally, there is no need to tell other people you are hustling. Just hustle and let the results represent the Hustle.

But there is something larger at play here that is more harmful than people bragging about their Hustle. Because of the Hustle mantra people are running around spending time, energy, and money with little regard to the purpose, direction, and results of their Hustle. It's easy to Hustle. Just be busy and share the busyness on social media. Now you are hustling and you have the pics to prove it. You might have even purchased a Hustle T-shirt, notebook, or sticker to represent your Hustle to others. But Hustle without intention, prioritization, and discipline is inconsequential. Hustle alone will wear you out and accomplish nothing . . . Hustle fatigue.

Discipline is the true measure of your ability to execute now on what matters most. Where Hustle represents the busy, discipline demands proper intention and action. Where Hustle invokes positivity and optimism, discipline ignores emotion and feelings to do what needs to be done most, right now. And then tomorrow, the next day, and in perpetuity. Discipline teaches us we don't have to like it and no one will probably know but us, but when we act in a disciplined manner over time, we are becoming a results juggernaut.

The challenge is that we are undisciplined as a species.

Here is how I know. I give a talk on building software products at conferences and to prove a point about people being undisciplined, even when we know the principles to something, I ask the audience if everyone agrees the keys to being fit and healthy (outside of disease or chronic illness) are to eat well and get consistent, strenuous exercise. Everyone agrees with these two principles to produce the outcome. Then I ask how many people are as fit and healthy as they want to be and one to two percent standup. I follow-up by asking the audience if they want to be fit and healthy and they all say yes. So they want the result; they know the two principles (that's it, two!), and yet they are too undisciplined to do it.

I've been fortunate to get to know many people across all walks of life. The most successful and happy ones are the most disciplined. Yes, being disciplined makes you not only productive, but also happy. The most successful people figure out what they want and why they want it. They know what they are willing to forgo to get it and then show up everyday to make it happen. Irrespective of what is happening around them or to them and how good or bad they feel. I've come to call this ruthless, daily level of discipline, "The Discipline of Execution."

The Discipline of Execution in one area of your life is good. Having the Discipline of Execution in all areas of your life is game-changing. You will accomplish more than you could have ever imagined and develop a confidence to take on new challenges and opportunities because you will have proven to yourself that you can execute, consistently, no matter what else is happening.

So how do you become more disciplined and less focused on things like Hustle? There are two key strategies you can start now. First, don't focus on getting as much as you can done in a day for the sake of volume. Instead, focus on getting the most important, highest value things done each day. The principle of three seems to work best. In the morning, before you get involved in doing anything, document the three things that are the most important for you that day. Maybe you will get all three done in that day, but what matters most is whether you know these are the three most important things and make progress in completing them that day. It also has gratefulness and affirmation aspects that we can all benefit from. I've found a journal (and App) to help with this piece everyday. It's called "The 5 Minute Journal." I have no stake in and do not benefit in anyway from referencing The 5 Minute Journal.

Second, do at least one thing everyday to prove to yourself you can be disciplined and to strengthen your discipline muscle. It has to be something that will challenge you and give you value for doing it. Showing up to work on time, letting someone into traffic, or waiting for the walk sign before crossing a street doesn't count. If you want to read more to expand your world or to learn something, then reading qualifies. So does eating well and exercising. Or learning to play an instrument or to speak a new language. Here is the secret. Whatever it is, and you can pick more than one, you must do it every day for 90 days. If doing more than one puts even one at risk, then only do one. If you can commit to and do more than one, then you will strengthen your discipline muscle that much faster and it will become that much stronger.

You're probably thinking doing something everyday for 90 days sounds like an unreasonable expectation. It's not. Don't set unrealistic expectations initially. It's one of the reasons people fail in remaining disciplined. They set the expectation they have to do something for at least an hour or longer for it to count. I don't know why we think this, but we do and it hampers our ability to be disciplined around things that matter. I recommend starting with 15 minutes per day. If you can do something meaningful for 15 minutes a day, for 90 days, you will become a more disciplined person.

Discipline is undeniable. Discipline breaks through barriers and overcomes obstacles. The most talented don't always win and don't always accomplish more than others in their field. But the most disciplined do. The New England Patriots do not have the most talented roster of players compared with other teams. However, the Patriots are the most disciplined team. They execute with greater discipline and that is the result of preparing with more discipline. The Patriots Discipline of Execution is what wins them championships, not superior talent.

The most successful Founders are the most disciplined. Yes, successful Founders are also smart, creative, etc., but one thing they have in common is being disciplined. Leave the Hustle mantra behind and be disciplined. Hustle will leave you exhausted, unfulfilled, and unaccomplished.

Discipline will help you accomplish more and in some cases things you never thought possible. Discipline produces results. The world respects and pays for results.

A big piece of discipline is prioritization. This is why focusing on the three highest priorities every day is so valuable.

Founders need to prioritize and execute their work ruthlessly. They also need to help the team. Everything matters in a startup, but everything doesn't matter equally today or even at this moment. Founders are flooded with issues, requests, and numerous things and people demanding their attention. The best Founders identify what matters most and then focus on those things before turning their attention to other things. We all have only so much time and energy to focus on and excel at things. Founders who get great at ruthless prioritization use their time and energy better than others.

Founders executing ruthless prioritization will also be establishing it as a core value and skill of the company and team. A team that values and is great at prioritizing will accomplish more of the most important things, faster. Note, it's more, faster. It's more of the important things, faster. Volume of work isn't the objective. It's the doing the right work, right now.

One of the challenges of prioritizing for Founders and startup teams is balancing what is easy and what is hard. Easy tends to look like adding an inconsequential feature to the product, adding a page to the site, finding new images for social channels, building for future scalability prematurely, and so on. Easy or hard is irrelevant. What matters most, right now, and will drive the most value should be what gets attention and therefore, worked on.

We live in a time of instant gratification. The urgency to produce results, quickly is greater for Founders than for most people. Speed matters in creating products and starting companies (more on this in *Chapter 33: Speed Matters*). Founders have to operate with discipline, while moving uncomfortably fast, but don't mistake this for instant gratification. There are short-term wins along the way, but Founders need to be focused on day-in, day-out execution, not some vanity and ego inflating thing that makes them feel good but is also mostly irrelevant to the company's progress. Founders looking for shots of adrenaline and ego boosts along the way are more focused on themselves than the company and will act undisciplined as a result. Discipline at its essence is acknowledging what is important and acting upon it in the face of a lot of other demands, distractions, and influences.

Discipline helps you fight and control urges that are unproductive and potentially harmful. It's easy for Founders to weaken through the process and to succumb to urges, especially during highly challenging times. Founders need releases and escapes to stay mentally, physically, and spiritually strong. Founders need to recharge to maintain energy, be alert, and to have stamina. How Founders recharge is the key. Founders that recharge through positive experiences rooted in the same level of discipline they have been operating on top of for the company, are less likely to be lured by urges that seem fun and that will recharge them, when in fact they will drain them and actually diminish their energy and stamina. Positive escapes can be a hobby a Founder finds enjoyable—one that provides them with a counter-balance to how they are naturally wired and to their existence as a Founder. If a Founder is typically pretty high-strung, hobbies and escapes that slow and calm them down will be the most beneficial in allowing them time to recharge and to see things differently. Founders who are naturally calm might benefit most from hobbies and escapes that are creative and that challenge them in new, unique ways. It's important to note, when I reference escapes, I mean positive ones. Escapes to recharge and to cleanse and to provide inspiration and clarity for Founders. I don't mean escapes that are destructive like turning to drugs, alcohol, or negative relationships.

The most powerful technique in executing with discipline is to say no to things. If a request isn't one of the three highest priorities, then you should decline doing it until it is. Yes, this means declining a lot of ambiguous coffee meetings and not scheduling needless internal meetings. The best Founders understand what matters most right now and put their heads down and address those things. In doing so they say no to a lot of other things and people. If you want to be disciplined and ultra-productive, say no, frequently.

## CHAPTER 5
# First, Best

One of the reasons being a Founder and starting a company is the most challenging professional endeavor anyone can take on is Founders often have to be the first and best at everything for the company. Founders have to be the first and best salesperson, product manager, marketer, and recruiter, to name a few. Even for the things Founders don't have to be the first and best for the company such as, legal and accounting, they still have to know and understand the principles of those areas and how they will impact the company. Founders cannot and should not acquiesce any key aspects of the company to anyone.

The challenge is most Founders don't start companies to be the first, best salesperson, product manager, or recruiter. Some Founders will come with no experience in any of these areas and will have to ramp up quickly. Founders have to be prepared for the intensity of learning new skills and adapting to many new roles, while building the plane in flight.

Of course one of the reasons Founders need to be the first, best in everything is because there may not be much of a team outside of the Founder to start and for some time thereafter. But it goes much deeper than that. Being a Founder (entrepreneur) is really being a problem solver. A startup will have a continuous, seemingly unending stream of problems.

To have all of the necessary context to solve the problems with the appropriate priority and urgency, Founders need to understand the implications across all areas of the company.

Founders who expect others to sell, recruit, or manage the product early on, will decrease rather than increase their odds of success. I've even seen Founders and startups outsource fundraising. I've also never seen it work beyond a few thousand dollars and with everyone disappointed in the process. It is frustrating and challenging for Founders to get up to speed on all of the crafts and roles necessary to get the company moving. Founders even might end up resenting the fact they have to be the first, best in all of these roles. The assignment and division of roles and responsibilities among founding teams can also cause frustration and resentment if there isn't alignment and agreement around the assignments. A Founder who feels forced to sell and doesn't buy into it will not be good at it. It's imperative that founding teams have complete alignment and agreement on operational assignments. Once a founding team has assigned operational areas the Founders each need to embrace and dive into their respective roles with full commitment and fervor. This might involve going to some workshops, taking some online classes, hiring a trainer or coach, and reading a ton about a particular discipline. Founders can't stay in learning mode too long though. Founders need to quickly start doing the craft and mixing learning with doing. Doing is the best teacher. Founders learning a new craft is akin to the evolution of the product and company with frequent, small iterations as they become more informed and knowledgeable. Founders will likely fail horrifically on their first couple of sales calls, product meetings, and recruiting calls. That's okay and it's normal. It's the Founders' ability to learn from it and apply what they've been learning along the way to improve in very short cycles that matters.

As the team and company grows Founders also need to be able to relinquish responsibilities to people more knowledgeable and experienced in specific areas. Because Founders need to be the first, best for most if not all areas of the company, they can become control freaks. Founders need to be aware of and control the desire to want to do everything when they no longer have to or should. Just because Founders are the ones who started the company, it doesn't mean they are the best ones to do certain functions in the company. I can't overstate how challenging a transition this can be for Founders. To go from doing everything and having to learn skills to be able to do everything, to passing the torch to others to do things, is not easy. A company's culture is also greatly impacted by the Founders' abilities to make this transition happen smoothly and to empower the team to ply their craft with independence and freedom. The flatter a company's organizational structure, the easier this transition will be. Companies that put an aggressive management hierarchy in place typically have Founders who are trying to maintain control and be involved in everything. This is counter-intuitive, but companies that have a flatter organizational structure actually are less control focused than companies with lots of management hierarchy.

Founders should be prepared and expect to wear all of the hats when they start a company, but also realize this is a temporary situation that will change and evolve in direct relation to the pace and scale of the company's growth.

## CHAPTER 6
# Be a Great Storyteller

Founders need to be great storytellers. I know some Founders will turn their noses up at this. Don't. Or do so to your own detriment. Being a great storyteller is an absolute necessity now for Founders. It really always has been, and now we are just consciously more aware of it.

A Founder's most important role from the moment the decision is made to start the company is to communicate why the company exists and the impact of the company's existence. This is the essence of every startup and every company for that matter, irrespective of size and scope. Founders have to be able to articulate the why of the company succinctly and clearly.

Great storytelling establishes an antagonist and a protagonist. In the case of starting a company, the problem the company is solving is the antagonist and the company is the protagonist. And the layers and nuances get added. The problem must be solved because of how it affects people, companies, the world. The company gets positioned as the unique hero that is capable and committed to solving the problem.

Everyone who engages with a startup in a meaningful way is making an irrational decision to do so. Joining a team is an irrational decision. Being a startup investor is an irrational decision. Being a startup customer is an irrational decision. So why do these people make a decision to do a mostly irrational thing? Because they get to a point of believing the risk is not only worth it, but if they don't take the risk based on the vision of a new reality, they could be missing out on something impactful.

Think about it. Every aspect of being a great Founder is about storytelling.

**Team**—recruiting a team is storytelling. And this is the most important audience a Founder will have to persuade. Everything else at a startup is a derivative of the team. The team's capabilities. The team's commitment to each other and solving the problem. The team's credibility with investors and early customers. Founders that can't tell a compelling story to potential team members about why the company exists and what it is going to accomplish will not be able to assemble the A-team needed to deliver on the promise.

**Customers**—early customers don't buy the early product. Early products are and should be crap. Early customers buy what can be, not what is. What the product could become. Early customers care about the problem getting solved and believe the vision of a new reality with the product and company in the future where their existence is dramatically improved.

**Investors**—are placing a bet on the team's potential to deliver to a level investors will get a significant return on their investment during a relatively short period of time. Persuading investors to fund your company is storytelling. A pitch deck is a novel. It's fiction until you start delivering and accomplishing things. The pitch deck and pitch become less fiction over time and eventually, in the best of cases, crosses a threshold to be more non-fiction. The best teams and the best companies don't get all of the investment. The Founders that can tell the story the best do. In ideal situations it all measures up.

**Partners**—do business with you not because of where you are with the company, but where you could be and the ability for you to be a difference maker for the partner. Partnering with a startup is of course also risky and most companies won't. The ones that do are doing so because they believe the future with the startup is better and more enticing than life without it. Often startup partnering is how companies innovate. Innovation isn't the pursuit of the probable, it's the pursuit of what is possible. Your company's possibilities and the ability to communicate it clearly and effectively is what makes partnerships happen.

**Advisors**—worth having as advisors want to provide value and have an impact. The best advisors want to advise Founders who are solving the most interesting and impactful problems that are also the most humble and coachable. Recruiting the best advisors you can for your company is about telling a compelling story that makes them want to share their expertise and experience with you versus others or not at all.

**Service Providers**—engaging with startups as a service provider is a risky and volatile existence. Service providers engage with startups because they get excited about being part of solving the problem and being part of the growth and success of the startup. This is mostly an emotional decision, not a logical one. For most service providers engaging with startups is not a sound business decision. There are other clients that would be much less volatile to do business with. Yet service providers do engage with startups that get them excited about what could be and being part of making it happen. This is storytelling through and through. The startups that work with the best service providers do so because the Founders are great storyteller's that also make service providers feel like they will have FOMO (Fear of Missing Out) if they don't. That's the power of great storytelling.

Being a great storyteller is no longer optional for Founders. Founders likely aren't great, natural storytellers which means they should hire a speaking or storytelling coach. A speaking and storytelling coach will pay for themselves multiple times over as the Founders engage with all key stakeholders around the company. I know some great speaking and storytelling coaches, if you would like an introduction to one, message me: ryan@thefoundersmanual.com.

**CHAPTER 7**
# The Rest of Your Life

If you are going to be a Founder I highly recommend having the rest of your life together as much as possible. Having your life together can encompass a lot and means different things to different people. I've seen many Founders not be the leaders they could be and not have the success available to them, because other aspects of their lives cause too much thrashing they couldn't overcome. Thrashing is destructive personally and professionally. Too much thrashing for too long for Founders will create an environment that is too negative and corrosive for building a company.

Here are some areas I believe are important to have in a reasonably stable state if you are going to take the startup journey as a Founder. These are probably also true for early startup team members. Take these with the caveat that conditions will never be perfect for you to start a company. You can always delay, waiting for some shoe to drop. The areas listed below will help make the journey of being a Founder easier and smoother, but not easy or smooth.

## Significant Other

Trying to get into and establish a meaningful and healthy personal relationship while you are also starting a company is a doubly challenging existence. I've seen Founders try to pull both off without much success. The company or the relationship, or both, suffer, and neither ends up being successful. Starting a company and being a Founder is much like starting a new personal relationship. A startup requires and demands similar attention and care to that of a new personal relationship. Maybe more. The company is unyielding and unsympathetic. The company needs what it needs, now. At least a new significant other can cut you some slack and be empathetic to what you are going through. 'Can be' being the operative words. Trying to get a new personal relationship off the ground while also trying to get a company off the ground divides your time, attention, and energy to a level that most people seeking a significant other are dissatisfied with. This doesn't make them a bad, selfish person. It's hard for anyone that isn't a Founder to relate to the all-encompassing journey being a Founder is. The other person will likely begin to resent the amount of time and attention the company gets as compared to what they get. This is natural. This also doesn't make you as a Founder a bad person. It just probably makes you not a great life partner for someone that is looking for a more normal existence and relationship.

If you are already in a relationship make sure you have open candid conversations about the journey on which you are about to embark and ensure you have alignment with your partner. There is no way for each of you to know precisely what the existence will be like if it is your first time being a Founder, but at least you can establish a foundation of communication and commitment to work through it as various complications arise. Starting a company without being aligned with your significant other is a recipe for disaster. Something is going to give. This often manifests with the significant other resenting how much time and focus is spent on the company. Turns out people in a relationship expect to be the number one priority and don't take kindly to being the second, third, or even lower priority. Resentment from the significant other can develop, creating a rift that can be hard to repair. Avoid as much of the resentment as possible by keeping the significant other aware of what is happening with you and the company all the time. They might not be able to relate to and understand what you are going through but the transparency and communication will demonstrate you care about their perspective and keeping them informed.

## Friendships

Being a Founder will create new friendships (albeit mostly around the business) and solidify or erode existing ones. Many young Founders, who are at a formative part of their lives including making and fortifying friendships, are conflicted between their social lives and their role as a Founder. Some of it is understandable and Founders should be intentional about growing and caring for every aspect of themselves, but Founders need to understand they are not only making a professional choice to start a company, but also a personal one—a personal one that will make it challenging to have and maintain an active social calendar and lifestyle. Founders will also likely experience many friendships devolving and some going away completely. This is a very difficult thing for Founders to deal with. Friendships ending, or at least not being as close, is never easy to go through.

This is one the leading causes of Founder loneliness referenced in Chapter 2: Self-awareness. The friends that really want to support you, will. These friends will put their own feelings aside and not make it about them, but about you. That doesn't mean that they will understand and be able to relate to what you are going through, but friends worth making time for as a Founder will support you irrespective of their level of understanding.

## Your Herd

Building on friendships from above, one of the reasons this matters so much when you are a Founder is because the people we spend the most time with have a significant impact on our attitude, perspectives, beliefs, and actions. I heard someone reference this recently as, "Your Herd." Replace that reference with any you prefer more—crew, squad, etc. Founders need to be very intentional about cultivating their herd to be made up of people who are supportive, positive, and understanding. Your herd does to an extent define you as a person and professionally as a Founder. I see a lot of Founders spending time and hanging out with the wrong herd for them. Founders should surround themselves with people who are intentional, disciplined, and accomplished. Founders hanging around other Founders and people who are unfocused and undisciplined results in more of the same by everyone involved. Founders need to level up their herd, even if it is uncomfortable. Leveling up your herd means spending time with people who are successful in their chosen fields and who think and see things differently than you do. I started to get to know successful speakers, authors, artists, and musicians in addition to my typical herd of product people, technologists, and investors. Discussing and learning how successful people from different crafts see, practice, and evolve their craft provides great insight on new ways for Founders to think about their perspective and approach. Your herd contributes to defining you, and as a Founder, you need to be running with the best herd you can find.

## Living arrangements

No one enjoys moving. Moving is time-consuming and stressful. Moving in the early stages of starting a company is a huge distraction. If you know you are going to be moving to either start the company or because of other factors, get the move over with before you dig in on the company. Especially in the early, formative days of a company, a distraction like moving has significant implications. In the case of moving to start the company somewhere else or to be part of an accelerator (more on accelerators in Chapter 25) you not only have the normal challenges of moving but the added challenges of learning a new area. I've seen many Founders uproot their lives to move to be part of an accelerator and although it sometimes proves beneficial, more often it isn't. Are some areas more conducive to starting a particular type of company? Sure, but unless you are starting a company that is dependent on some external resources and factors that are critical to success, most companies can be started anywhere and succeed anywhere. To the greatest extent possible Founders should be stable with their living situation so they don't have to deal with complications around it and can focus on the company. Even unstable and inconsistent roommate situations can be enough of a distraction and stressor to affect a Founder's ability to focus on the company as needed.

## Financially

It is incredibly difficult to start a company when you're heavily in debt. Not impossible and we've all heard the stories of $500 becoming a $50 million company. These stories are anomalies. In most cases it is going to take some money to get a company started and to support its operations. Depending on the type of company, product, or industry, it is true that it has never been easier and less expensive to start a company. However, it is also true that it has never been harder and more expensive to make a company successful. Marketing and customer acquisition costs continue to rise for example. Founders don't have to be wealthy, but starting a company while heavily in debt is having the odds stacked against you, not in your favor. Every Founder has heard the narrative around friends and families funding to get a company started. The rub is most Founders don't have friends and family to raise money from. The fact is, more companies get funded initially through credit cards than any other mechanism. Credit card issuers are the largest segment of early stage funding for startups. Founders don't need great credit to get venture funding, but Founders should have some ability to get access to some purchasing power when starting a company. This could be through credit cards or refinancing real estate or a second mortgage, but to think a company is going to be able to get started without access to capital, even highly leveraged and expensive capital, is probably naive.

## Health

Founders who are reasonably fit and healthy typically have more stamina and resiliency. One of my favorite books is *The Power of Agency* by Paul Napper and Anthony Rao. I liked it because it is principle-based, but also because Founders need a lot of Agency, so it was very relatable. A big piece of Agency for Founders comes from physical and mental well being. I focus more on mental health in other areas of the book. Founders who maintain physical fitness and health increase their Agency. It's important to note I am talking about physical fitness and health at a reasonable level for a generally healthy person. I've met countless Founders who have some physical limitations and challenges, as well as Founders with diseases that impact their physical well being and these Founders typically already have Agency as part of their journey to deal with the physical limitations and disease affects. The benefits of a Founder being fit and healthy for whatever that means for them are enormous. Founders, just like anyone, have a better capacity to deal with mental and emotional stresses if they are getting regular, strenuous physical exercise. Founders who are healthy also are more confident and lucid in important moments of decision making, leadership, and interactions with key stakeholders.

## Sleep

The hustle mantra has driven us into a frenzy and the belief around being a Founder is that if you aren't working 12-hour days or more you are a slacker. This couldn't be further from the truth or more detrimental to Founders. No one can perform at their best without adequate, consistent sleep. I could have included sleep with health above, but I believe it merits being called out specifically. Being sleep deprived is not a badge of honor. Being well rested and reenergized is smart and productive. I would encourage Founders and really anyone to take naps during the day. A nap during the day restores us for the balance of the day to be more alert, creative, and thoughtful.

## Eating

Founders who are conscious of what they eat and in what portions are better equipped to deal with the demands of being a Founder. From a constant stream of problems and decisions, to an unusual schedule, Founders who put good things in their bodies are better able to cope and execute well. Founders should eat high-energy producing foods that fuel their bodies and minds and that don't cause the negative physical and emotional affects of being sluggish, tired, and crashing.

## Alcohol and drugs

I like bourbon and some of this book was written while I was drinking some. So I'm not sitting in some ivory tower casting judgment over Founders that drink booze or do drugs. But I have seen too many Founders that consume alcohol or drugs to an unhealthy, unproductive, and sometimes destructive level. Being a Founder can be a lonely and intense existence. There is constant stress and pressure to not only succeed, but to even survive. And it's all personal. The company is the Founder. Many Founders don't have positive outlets and ways of dealing with the stress and pressure so they turn to alcohol or drugs. It's also hard for Founders to see the signs of alcohol or drug use becoming addictive and having a negative influence on their mental state, emotions, and decision making. Founders need to be mindful of their alcohol or drug consumption. The Founder and CEO of Startup Grind and Bevy Labs, Derek Andersen, doesn't drink coffee or alcohol and I respect him for that. Derek is one of the best Founders I know in part because of his clear-mindedness and measured approach. Derek doesn't get too high or too low and is seemingly always under control. He also grinds (yes, pun intended) harder than most Founders and for that matter, most people. Derek said to me once, "I will hold my breath longer than anyone else," about his work ethic and competitiveness. Only Derek knows how much of his ability to perform at a high-level for long periods of time is a result of his foregoing coffee and alcohol, but the results are unquestionable. I'm not saying you can't and shouldn't have fun, but because of the mercurial journey that is being a Founder, this is a slippery slope for many. Founders feeling an increased level of stress and anxiety that is beginning to feel unmanageable should seek support and guidance from medical and psychological professionals. As I reference above in Chapter 2: Self-awareness, Founders benefit greatly by regularly seeing a mental wellness therapist to help them deal with the demands of the journey.

## Don't be cool and in the know

Founders should not expect to remain cool and in the know. As Founders limit their inputs and filter what they are allowing into their minds, they need to get comfortable with FOMO (fear of missing out) to the point of not caring about it or paying attention to it. Being a successful Founder takes that kind of focus and energy. There is no room for staying up on current events, the latest shows, and cultural happenings. Founders need ways to unplug and recharge, but doing so in ways that do not clutter their minds and actually help to cleanse their minds is best. Founders getting away and unplugging is actually far more beneficial than plugging into activities and content that in the end is just noise.

I could probably add another ten elements to this Principle. I won't. The ones referenced above are the ones that carry most of the weight and importance, beyond being self-aware in Chapter 2. Being a Founder is a mentally, emotionally, and physically demanding experience. Don't make it harder than it already is.

CHAPTER 8
# Convicted Flexibility

Being a Founder is a mercurial and often lonely journey. Founders discover there are countless people wanting to meet with them to give them advice, to sell them services, or to give their opinion on why the Founder is crazy, why the company won't work, why the company will work under certain circumstances, and a host of other things. Founders need to be highly selective from whom they take advice. With this onslaught of advice, Founders need to remain convicted and committed to why they are intent on solving the problem and steadfast in doing so.

## Advice

Founders should only take advice from people that have done what the Founder is trying to do or from area specialists. Taking advice from well-respected and startup-knowledgeable legal, financial, and product people makes sense. These areas of specialization cut across most companies and products. Founders would never be able to get to the level of experience and expertise as these professional advisors in the timespan needed. Beyond these professional advisors I still see too many Founders seeking and taking advice from inexperienced and uninformed people. Founders are susceptible to these so-called advisors because they can be naive, scared, lonely, and more. And these so-called advisors are typically not working in the best interest of the Founders. They are working in their best interest of getting paid, getting equity, or both. One way Founders demonstrate convicted flexibility to themselves and others is by embracing, learning from, and heeding the advice of professionals while discounting and ignoring irrelevant advisors.

## Choosing Lines

I think a lot about approaches and ways to navigate things—intangible and intellectual things as well physical and tangible things. In fact, I'm launching a casual apparel company for outdoor adventure enthusiasts called LINE Apparel Co. I'm starting LINE to pay homage to picking the right line when doing an outdoor adventure activity such as mountain biking, snowboarding, or surfing, among others. Choosing the right line when riding something on a trail, slope, or surf is paramount to doing it safely and quickly. The best outdoor adventure athletes know how to choose the best lines. I see a lot of similarities between being an outdoor adventure athlete and a Founder. Founders also need to be good at choosing the best lines as part of the company progressing and succeeding. Choosing the best line on a trail and in a startup both take reading the environment, the current conditions, and then making a very fast decision of where to head. A big difference between choosing a line as Founder, compared to an outdoor adventure athlete, is that Founders are likely navigating situations and circumstances they've never encountered before. This of course can be true for new outdoor adventure athletes and outdoor adventure athletes taking up a new outdoor adventure activity.

## Angles

Getting good at choosing the right line in an outdoor adventure activity and a startup is understanding and being able to read angles. Angles are an under-appreciated aspect of sports, business, and life. You will hear sports announcers talk about angles being missed or leveraged when a big play happens. The best at every sport understand angles extremely well. In some cases it's more instinctual and in some cases learned. The highest performing athletes combine both. It's obvious when watching a game which players understand and are able to leverage angles. A goalie comes far out from the goal to look and be as big as possible, cutting down the angle. A receiver in football catches the ball at the highest point to make it harder for the defensive player to get to the ball.

## Force

The world tells us to hustle and to grind. These sentiments are not bad unto themselves, but as I discuss in Chapter 4: Discipline, about discipline being far more important than hustle, they can create a mindset that is unproductive. One of the ways this can be seen is in the amount and intensity of force Founders apply to a startup and their work. The universe repels force with direct and equal force. I see many Founders who have the mindset that if they just worked longer and harder, somehow they will break down and break through the walls in front of them and the company.

Founders who continue to bang their head against the wall thinking if they just bang more and harder that somehow the wall is going to get smaller or softer don't understand the laws of force.

## Escape hatches

You can spot an uncommitted and non-convicted Founder when you see escape hatches they've brought into play and keep alive. The escape hatches take the form of not fully committing to the company by not working in the company full-time, taking side gigs while supposedly working on the company full-time, and taking shortcuts in critical areas that are positioned as being in the best interest of the company when it is known they are not. Founders who are not all in will even subconsciously create escape hatches, you know in case things don't work out. This never ends well for anyone. Starting and growing a company is challenging enough and the odds of success are so low even in the best of circumstances that having any escape hatches is an inevitable outcome. Plan B's, C's, and D's are not necessarily bad inside the dynamics of navigating the potential paths of a company, but strategic directions and choices are not escape hatches. I've seen a lot of chatter about whether Plan B's are good or bad. They are bad if not inside the context of strategic options for the company. Plan B's and beyond for Founders personally mean certain death for the company. The irresponsible part is some Founders don't make their team, investors, customers, or partners aware they have a personal Plan B and then when the Founder decides to use the escape hatch everyone else is caught off guard. Founders need to work on their business full-time once the decision has been made that there is a problem worth solving and the Founder is committed to building a company to solve it. Building a company of consequence is not a side hustle. It's not a try scenario. It's a do scenario. Trying is what you do when you aren't committed to something and when you have escape hatches. Doing is what you do when you are serious and committed. Be a doer, not a trier. Leave escape hatches behind you for your pre-Founder days. If you are the kind of person that likes a lot of options you've got some work to do to get in the right mindset to be a Founder.

## Convicted flexibility

Convicted flexibility is my representation of the mindset Founders should have to stay grounded and intentional about why they started their companies combined with the ability to be flexible in the face of new and better information. It's easy for Founders to be convicted when they first start the company, but that becomes increasingly harder as more people get involved and the business gets more complex. Founders who become unyielding in the face of new and better information about the company, the product, the market, and anything else are defending an old position that might have had its place in time to be defended, but now has to evolve for the company to progress.

## CHAPTER 9
# Emotional Quotient

A Founder's ability to be empathetic, while dealing with intense business challenges and relationships is important in order to overcome challenges and to build solid relationships. The higher a Founder's EQ (emotional quotient, i.e. intelligence) the better the Founder's ability to get all the challenging things done inside of often unreasonable circumstances and expectations. By being able to understand and relate with key people as part of the journey, they are more likely to overcome seemingly insurmountable conditions and execute well. The only way to accomplish immensely challenging things is to do it in a highly respectful, communicative, and collaborative way.

## Team
Founders recruit, and depending on the growth pace of the company stay involved in recruiting the team for a while, as they should. Being part of the recruitment of the team gives Founders the ability to connect with team members from the very inception of their interactions with the company. Establishing an early connection gives Founders and team members time to develop a mutually empathetic relationship and understanding. This mutually high EQ relationship serves all well during surely difficult situations. Founders

know they can speak and operate with candor and team members know it is coming from a place of respect and value.

## Customers

There is an old adage in sales that customers don't care about what you are selling until they know how much you care about them. This goes well beyond sales. For Founders, the empathy and ability to relate with customers and their state is everything in getting them to take a chance with the product and company. Being an early customer of a startup is a mostly irrational decision. A Founder's ability to understand and then be empathetic to a customer's situation is the bridge that provides comfort for customers making the irrational decision to engage with a startup.

## Investors

Investing in startups is also a mostly irrational endeavor. Most startups won't provide a return great enough to pay the investors back with enough upside to warrant the investment. From Angel Investors up to the largest Venture Capital firms, multiple investments are made because investors know the stats and their experience of how many companies they need to invest in to have confidence at least one will provide a return large enough to cover all of the investments made during a period. Founders need to understand the existence and realities of investors and then be able to manage their EQ with investors. Many Founders don't understand the business and realities of being a venture investor. Founders who attempt to raise funding without understanding and being empathetic to the what investors deal with, will likely not raise funding. Founders who do, increase their chances of raising funding dramatically. Founders seeking funding need to spend the time understanding venture investing and then demonstrating their understanding, empathetically with investors.

## Partners

Inevitably there will be partnerships important to the company. Around the product, data, marketing, sales, distribution, etc. Founders, especially early on, will be the initiators and stewards of the partnerships. The best partnerships are mutually respectful, valued, and balanced. Establishing great partnerships is as much about mutual understanding and empathy as anything else. Of course, the business terms must work and be agreeable, but once that's the case, it's about how well you respect and support each other that matters. Founders need to understand their partners' motives and circumstances to develop and foster mutually valuable partnerships that are sustainable.

## Get assessed

Some investors are now asking for and in some cases even requiring EQ assessments and training for Founders they are considering investing in and those they already have if it becomes clear that improvement is needed. Similarly, many Founders and startups are requesting EQ assessments of potential new team members as part of the recruiting process. I encourage Founders to take an EQ assessment and potentially seek training on their own. Having a high EQ is vitally important for all of the key relationships that a

Founder must build and maintain. For some Founders, having a low EQ could be an obstacle to being successful. EQ is something that can be assessed and improved. Founders should not leave it to chance, given all the other aspects of a company over which they will have little control.

CHAPTER 10

# Recruiting

The team is everything. It's not just a narrative, like many, that gets parroted because we think that is what is supposed to be said. In this case, it's true!

One of a Founder's most important roles is recruiting. Given the importance of the team, I still see some Founders not embracing the need to focus on their key role in building the team. Yes, recruiting and building the team can be messy and complicated. Turns out, people can be messy and complicated and building the team requires a lot of people-interaction skills.

Founders need to put themselves in the shoes of potential team members to be able to empathize with their positions. Assuming Founders are building the most committed and capable team they can, potential team members that fit this description will most likely be plying their craft somewhere they enjoy working. As much as Founders need to believe the company they are building is a place really smart and skilled people want to work, there are a lot of professional and personal factors that go into where we ply our crafts. Founders that seek to deeply understand a potential team member's current situation, their professional objectives, and their personal drivers, are in a much better position to be relatable and have a higher chance of recruiting the teams they need. Just as you can't effectively sell a potential customer on buying without understanding the problem deeply and the customer's pain and desires around the problem, you can't expect to recruit sought-after team members without understanding their situations and motives.

Attracting highly skilled talent has never been more competitive than it is now. People with high-value skills have the ability to pick from many opportunities. Make no mistake, the team members you want and need are highly desirable and have many options beyond your company. To win, Founders need to be great storytellers describing a new reality of how potential team members will be part of an amazing journey and team solving a problem worth solving. The best way I've seen to recruit team members is by focusing on the problem and why the problem has to be solved, now, and by this company and team. Smart, capable people want to have an impact. They want to solve problems. The bigger the impact of solving a consequential problem, the more gratification they get out of their work.

Just as Founders need to keep their egos under control, so do the rest of the team. To this end, I have spoken to a lot of Founders and recruiters recently who put humility at the top of their candidate attribute list. This is also sometimes referred to as the "no asshole" rule. Not surprisingly, having a bunch of egomaniacs around isn't great for culture or productivity. Understanding someone's humility and ego during the interview process isn't easy but Founders and recruiters are beginning to uncover some ways to gracefully and tactfully assess it. A Founder who is building an incredible team recently told me he is uncovering humility and ego by digging deeper on a candidates involvement and contribution to projects they've been involved in. Candidates that focus only or mostly on their contribution and refer to themselves frequently as "I did this" and "I did that" as part of the project are demonstrating an ego-centric perspective, whereas candidates that can articulate their role and contribution but who also acknowledge and give credit to the rest of the team are comfortable with their impact without making it all about them and discounting the role of others. It's important to filter out any ego maniacs and to not let any into the team. A high-performer who is toxic, is not a high-performer.

**CHAPTER 11**

# Ego

Do you need to have an ego as a Founder? I would posit more that you need to be committed and confident. But that could be regarded as semantics, so yes, let's say you need to have an ego that drives your belief that you can build a team, product, and company to solve a high-value problem you care about.

With the above in mind, no one cares that you are the Founder. And the product doesn't care. The best Founders are the people that see the opportunity to solve the problem as a privilege and they honor the privilege by always working in the best interest of solving the problem most efficiently and effectively.

Founders who seek too much personal attention and focus eventually become a celebrity Founder. I met a Founder a few years ago that was struggling to get traction. When I asked him if he was having success anywhere, he said they had signed several customers in a specific space. I asked him why he wasn't doubling down on this area and he said it didn't align with his vision of what he wanted the company to do and be about. I told him he was letting his ego get in the way and that he was protecting his ego by focusing on what the company should be versus what customers wanted and valued. This Founder ended up shutting the company down. This is a clear and classic example of a Founder being ego driven. Since what customers really wanted wasn't cool enough for the Founder, the Founder protected his ego versus operating in the best interest of the company. Founders have to have a vision but if the vision is based on a Founder's ego the company has almost no chance of succeeding and if it does it will be short-lived.

I see a lot of ego-driven Founders pursuing individual recognition and acknowledgment. This frequently manifests through the pursuit of being part of media company lists. You know the kind—20 over 20, 30 under 30, future 50, and 6 over 60. I dislike these lists. I dislike them for several reasons. I get that media companies need content. These lists are viewed as unique content for media companies, events, and publications because everyone's list is going to be different even if they are rating and ranking the same thing. The media companies also know they will get some built-in promotion and marketing as part of doing the lists. What's the first thing that happens when a list is announced? Everyone who is on the list starts sharing it and promoting the list and their inclusion. The posts usually start with something like, "I'm humbled," "I'm honored," "I'm privileged." The media company gets the eyeballs and clicks they were after. The listees get their ego massaged. And what does it all mean? What does it matter? Nothing, that's what; it really doesn't matter at all. I've seen Founders lobby and work harder to get included on lists than on their product or company. Customers don't care if you are on a list. Investors don't care. Neither do team members. The only one who cares is you. And if you care too much about it, you are being driven by your ego and are not working in the best interest of the company and its stakeholders. Whenever it becomes more about you, the Founder, you should stop, re-evaluate what you are doing or about to do and change course.

Being a Founder doesn't automatically make you a leader. I see a lot of Founders that think it does. Being a Founder is being an initiator and a catalyst. Being a leader is finding and empowering others to care as much, if not more, about the cause than you do and for them to apply their skills and time in pursuit of the cause.

If you feel the need to be right, you might not want to be a Founder. You are wrong way more as a Founder than you are right. People that have the need to be right find being a Founder an aggravating and frustrating experience. New, first-time Founders believe they are supposed to be right and that the team, customers, partners, and investors always expect them to be right. This isn't the case and it takes time to figure it out, with some never realizing it. A stubborn Founder who has to be right and who digs in to defend a position, their position, to be right isn't a leader and isn't someone anyone wants to interact with over any length of time. Rather than being focused on being right, Founders should be focused on *what* is right, not *who* is right. What is right, might be far away from where the Founder starts on a particular point but by being open-minded and willing to consider often more informed positions from team members and others, Founders can actually be right more often. Founders should guard against forming a position on a problem too early and then being forced to defend the position, even in the face of new, better information. Doing what is right is more important than being right.

A derivative of being ego driven and the need to be right is being a control freak. This is another aspect of being a Founder many misunderstand and get wrong. It's a delicate balance to strike between being accountable for what happens and trying to control everything that happens. Founders are ultimately accountable for everything that happens with the company and this causes many to equate that with needing to control everything. Needing to and attempting to control everything isn't being a leader and isn't empowering the team. Control is something we seek when we feel inferior or insecure. A Founder who has recruited a talented and committed team should feel neither of these. Talented and committed team members won't last long working with a control freak. Being a control freak also inhibits the company's ability to evolve and grow. A Founder who is a control freak is instituting a real and perceived decision-making bottleneck. Having all key decisions flow through the Founder makes an ego-driven and insecure person feel validated, which perpetuates the problem. Of course, there are situations where a Founder has to step in to provide direction and to make the final call on a decision, but the team will know this is being done for the sake of progress and decisiveness, not control.

Envy is different than ego, but it's important to mention. Founders who are envious of other Founders and company success are on a disappointing and destructive path. Early in my so-called career (I recorded a podcast a few years ago and the host asked me to describe my career journey. I laughed and said, "I don't think you can call what I've done a career in the true sense of the term.") I was having a conversation with the lead investor, and I was waxing poetic, okay whining, about how another company had more resources, more funding, seemingly more of everything than we did. He stopped smoking his cigar, looked me as if he was going to kill me and then said, "Don't ever be jealous of someone else's cookie jar." He went on to say, "The time and energy you spend thinking about their cookie jar is a waste. It doesn't help your cookie jar be any fuller. Focus on your own cookie jar and if you aren't satisfied with it, do something about it. People that pay attention to their own cookie jars, end up with the best cookie jars." I have never forgotten this conversation around envy. Founders need not worry about and think about anyone else's cookie jar. There is plenty of work to be done for Founders to be satisfied with their own cookie jars.

Speaking of being satisfied with cookie jars ... this turned out to be a lot of work for me and it might be for other Founders, too. I once told someone I was perpetually dissatisfied. The other person was taken aback and I dug in around it. I mean I was, and I wore it as a badge of honor. I thought being perpetually dissatisfied was fuel. It helped drive me and keep me hungry, pushing for more and for better. It was my insurance policy against becoming complacent and average. Yuck, average. Being average and normal were horrific concepts and existences for me. Average and normal aren't interesting to me; average counters my idea of being alive. There seemed to be a vast difference between people who were living and those that were alive. Being alive meant to not give in to and to avoid being average and normal. I still have the perspective I don't want to be normal and to live a normal existence, but now it is grounded in being about me and what I want, not being envious about what else someone is doing or has. Being dissatisfied can be fuel and can drive you to get better, but Founders have to be mindful it is about them and no one else. Founders also have to balance their current level of dissatisfaction with recognition of what they have accomplished, how they've improved, and to be grateful for it all. Here's to your cookie jar running over with all of your favorite cookies!

Founders can keep their egos in check by reminding themselves they are never as great as their best moments and never as bad as their worst moments. There will be plenty of both along the way and the Founders that can remain even-keeled throughout have a better chance of succeeding. When good things happen Founders should celebrate, but it should never be a celebration about them. It should be focused on the team and the accomplishment, not a time to inflate the Founder's ego or search for Founder validation. When less than ideal things happen, the Founder should seek to understand what happened, why things didn't work out as expected, how to correct it, move forward, and then move on. A Founder dwelling on and getting caught up in something that didn't go well is often more about the Founder trying to save face or defend a now-failed decision. Acknowledge it, learn from it, and move on. Don't make the wins or losses about you. In fact, don't make anything about you.

## CHAPTER 12
# Long Game, Immediate Focus

Founders need to play the long game, while maintaining a hyper, immediate focus to make sure daily, even momentary, progress is being made. The goal after all is to build a sustainable, successful business, not some temporary, wiz-bang startup.

Playing the long game while maintaining a hyper focus on what is happening right now is incredibly challenging. This often feels like a contradiction and Founders can feel very hypocritical. One minute Founders are urging the team to deal with a high priority, immediate issue and the next telling the team to step back and think about the long-term implications of an issue and decision. This balance can make Founders go crazy, but it is a balance they need to strike. Knowing what has long-term implications that can't be taken lightly and what can be acted on immediately is a critical skill for Founders to develop and have.

One such issue that comes up often for Founders, especially early on, is a customer wanting customization of the product to their requirements, specifications, and processes. If the customer is willing to pay for the customizations and is willing to allow the additional functionality to be used by other customers, essentially relinquishing any rights to ownership of the code and product they are paying for, it makes the decision even more challenging. Landing the customer and revenue is of course very appealing. Extending and enhancing the product is too. In situations like this Founders have to step back and take all of the factors of saying yes into account. If the changes to the product are truly customizations—only the one customer will use them because of the customizations being so aligned with their specific processes and requirements—the likelihood of another customer wanting to use the functionality is low, if not zero. If other customers can't benefit from and use the additional functionality the value to you goes down dramatically. Another consideration is how you can incorporate the customizations technically into the product. If the product can't yet technically support the customizations inherently in the product and it is going to force the creation and implementation of a separate version or a Frankenstein version it may not be worth it. Situations like this that create what is called technical debt (technical debt is technical architecture and decisions around the way a product is developed that are not viable for long-term use) need to be taken very seriously as they have significant long-term consequences that aren't always readily apparent. Although acquiring a customer and feeling like the product got bigger and better for the customer as a result of the customizations can be enticing, these situations almost never make sense to say yes to. Saying yes to these kinds of situations is all short-term thinking and no long-term thinking.

Yes, Founders need to move fast. Uncomfortably fast for most, but moving fast doesn't mean ignoring long-term implications and ramifications. Burn rate is a hot topic and point of analysis for startups—mostly for those that have raised venture capital. Burn rate is how much money a startup is spending each month to operate. It includes all expenses for the company and money being spent. Payroll, office, software, marketing and everything else. Founders need to be very mindful of how the investment gets spent and to control the company's burn rate because if they burn hot and run out of money faster than expected they may not be able to raise more investment in time to keep operating. Remember the goal here is to build a successful company, not to see how fast the company can consume and go through money. Founders will often get mixed messages around the consumption and use of investment funds, even from their investors. Investors will tell Founders to use the funds as aggressively and quickly as possible. The positioning is usually, "We wrote you a check for you to use, now use it and fast." And as maybe can be predicted, when things start not to go well, investors are some of the first people to start to question the use of funds and burn rate. Founders need to manage to their pro forma as detailed more in *Chapter 18: Manage to Pro Forma*, and the pro forma should be reviewed and aligned with investors and the board frequently. It is the Founder's responsibility to manage funds of the company to execute the short-term plan, with understanding and an eye to the company's longer-term financial state. I've seen hundreds of startups burn through investment with no other path to funding; at this point, the company is dead. Investors can also be culprits in allowing this to happen. I have seen investors say to Founders they will lead or at least intend to invest in the next round of funding only to not do so. In some cases the investors were just stringing the Founders along and either had no intention of investing again, let alone leading the round or if they did, not making the Founders aware that circumstances have changed that won't allow them to continue investing. Telling a Founder they are going to invest and then not following through is irresponsible and performing professional malpractice. I've experienced this and have seen many other Founders experience it. In playing the long game and working in the best interest of the company, Founders need to manage investor relations and conversations expecting the investment to not happen until it happens and maintaining active, ongoing conversations with multiple investors. No sale with a prospective customer, no partnership, no team member recruitment, and no investment is done until it's done. Founders need to work accordingly.

Founders are confronted by a constant stream of decisions to make and often without enough or at least a comfortable amount of information to make the decisions. As a result, Founders have to make a lot of decisions in less than ideal circumstances. Many of the decisions are also part of negotiating something. There are countless negotiations for Founders to deal with. Some are significant with great consequences and some are minor with seemingly low consequences. Founders need to be able to recognize the difference and they also need to be able to determine which things need to be negotiated now and which things can wait for a stronger negotiating position. This is one of the occasions where a little bit of procrastination can be useful.

Not making a decision is making a decision. Not making a decision because the timing isn't right or because waiting on the decision as part of a negotiation makes sense, is a strategy. Sometimes negotiations call for playing the long game. When you have time and circumstances on your side as a Founder, leverage them as much as you can because it feels like this happens very rarely, especially early on in a company's evolution. Startups are high-risk and volatile, and vendors, customers, and partners will use this to negotiate deals that are one-sided to their advantage. It's appropriate for Founders to delay decisions when they are in the weaker position until their position improves. Often Founders will find that doing this makes them more desirable and the other party may reduce some of its demands as part of the negotiation. Sometimes the best approach is to play the long game in a negotiation and to wait the other part out or least force them to rethink their position.

Founders need to maximize today, really every moment, but also realize that each moment is one moment in time amongst a lot of moments in the company's life. A Founder's ability to maintain a grounded perspective as things are flying at them is critical. Many things that initially appear fatalistic turn out not to be. Minor things that are disregarded and discounted can result in a thousand cuts that ultimately do prove to be fatal. Everything matters, it just doesn't matter equally, right now. Founders have to be able to assess what matters most right now, then act on it, all the while keeping the big picture in mind—a long game approach with immediate focus and execution.

## CHAPTER 13

# Introverts

I'm an introvert so I'm admittedly biased on this. With that caveat, my experience tells me introverts make better, more successful Founders than extroverts do. All is not lost if you are an extroverted Founder, but it probably takes a bit more work.

### Observers

Introverts are great observers. They develop heightened observational skills while they sit in the back, stand in the corner, and are quiet. They let others step forward, presumably extroverts, and they watch what happens. They watch, take in and process everything. They watch how people act and react. They watch how the dynamic in the environment changes. They watch to see what the results of it are. After a while introverts get good at predicting who is going to do what, what the reaction is going to be, and what the outcomes will be. Being a great observer has immense value. A Founder is always observing, interpreting, predicting, redirecting and starting again. It all starts with problem identification. Because of evolved observational skills introverts tend to be able to identify and recognize problems more readily than extroverts. While extroverts are busy being seen, introverts are observing and seeing what others don't.

## Readers of people

Because introverts are extremely observant they develop the ability to read people and situations better than others. The ability to read people well is an invaluable skill as a Founder. It helps in every interpersonal interaction including with the team, investors and customers. I now believe introverts make the best salespeople because of their ability to read people and circumstances. From years of observing people and situations, introverts pick up on, process, and understand verbal, facial, and body queues on the fly. An introvert who has honed this skill to the highest level can even begin to predict how someone is going to react and what they are going to say. As a result, introverts are great at anticipating and reacting to the ebbs and flows of interactions and adjusting their course accordingly. Introverts will probably prepare diligently for an interaction and have a framework for the interaction in their mind, but also have the dexterity and comfort to go wherever the interaction takes them. Extroverts often take more of a wing-it approach because they falsely believe their personality will win out and carry the interaction. When the winging doesn't work, extroverts unlike introverts, are left scrambling to figure out what to do and say next.

## Out Front

Introverts of course can struggle with being the center of attention and putting themselves out there. They feel exposed and vulnerable. Introverts just want to go to work. Introverts don't want and don't seek the limelight. This can cause some internal conflict for introverts as Founders. Founders need to step forward to lead and to be the face and voice of the company. Introverts that can't make the transition to be out front and be effective at it will struggle with the responsibilities they hold. Introverted Founders can be more comfortable being a focal point as part of a founding team where the outward-facing responsibilities can be distributed across the founding team. This lessens the intensity on any one Founder to be the point person.

## Not without ego

It is often thought that introverts don't have egos or at least not as large as extroverts. Of course every person is different, but this isn't necessarily the case. An introvert's ego can manifest in different ways and areas than an extrovert's, but introverts certainly do have egos. Introverts' egos can often be centered around things like the need to be right, being uncompromising, and holding grudges. The things that make introverts different from extroverts can also be the introvert's greatest weakness. Introverts have the ability to be very empathetic given their observational and people-reading skills, and this can equate to the extroverts being great leaders as long as they keep their weaknesses around having to be right in check and begin to develop the ability to compromise.

## People like working with introverted Founders

People like working with introverts because they know introverts are grinders and will go to work on their behalf with an almost maniacal approach to the work. They know introverted Founders will lack some outward facing pizazz and will need to improve in this, but the grinding matters more. People also know that introverts will do whatever needs to be done and they are far less likely than extroverts to be diva's. Founders who are introverts naturally dig in to do and help wherever they are needed, when they are needed. Introverted Founders are more likely to know how most things in the company are performed because they've done each thing themselves, many times. They know how the trade show booth gets setup; they know how customers get invoiced; they know what the product roadmap is and how it gets created. They know it all because they have done it all. This evolves over time as the team and company grows, but early on introverted Founders earn the respect they value for being a grinder and sound operator.

Although it appears to be counter-intuitive that introverts would have qualities that can make them better Founders, it is often the case. Introverts still have a lot of work to do to leverage their unique qualities and to augment as needed, but their foundation is solid and often provides a better foundation for being a Founder than for those who are extroverts.

## CHAPTER 14
# Order

Among the frenetic pace of starting a company, Founders need to find ways to bring order. This can be challenging for many Founders because Founders aren't typically wired for order and routine. Founders value independence and freedom. That's part of the reason to be a Founder in the minds of many. That isn't all bad but being a successful Founder is more about establishing and maintaining order than most Founders initially realize.

### Routines

Routines are often frowned upon as boring and uninteresting, but routines can bring order in important aspects of the lives of Founders. Routines that free Founders to be able to think and to have fewer things to deal with provide significant value. The mundane things get taken care of easily and without much energy and thought. The time blocking and discipline that come from routines help Founders to better prioritize personally and professionally. The more Founders can make the basic aspects of daily living routine, the more productive they will be for the challenges coming their way.

Many years ago I started the routine of getting my clothes for the next day prepared the night before. It frees me from having to think about what I am going to wear in the morning, which means it makes it easier and faster for me to hit the ground running when I wake up. I also eat the same thing for breakfast every weekday so I have another thing I don't have to think about as I'm starting the day. Routines should be viewed as empowering, not limiting. Founders have more demands on their time than most people, increasing the need for and value of routines. Routines help Founders stay balanced across the spectrum of demands. To stay balanced Founders need to take care of the mind, body, and soul. Making the time for all of these areas consistently isn't possible without some level of routine. Making time for reading, exercising, and quiet, get intentionally accomplished best through routine. Read, exercise, and be quiet at the same time every day and soon what starts as a routine becomes a habit. Routines build habits that foster discipline. Founders need to simplify their lives and work whenever and wherever they can. Establishing routines is a great way to do it. When people wonder and remark about how someone appears to get more done in a day than others, I can say with great confidence that the person is leveraging some routines that allow them to get more done than other people. Founders should not discount routines; in fact they should embrace and implement as many as possible.

## Journaling

One of the ways for Founders to bring order to their lives is to journal. As mentioned elsewhere, I use a daily journaling app (there is also a paper notebook available) called Five Minute Journal. It isn't an extensive journaling exercise, but it is enough for me to make sure I am reflecting on and documenting the highlights of every day and my perspective around them. Journaling provides a way for Founders to get out of their own heads and provides a release. Journaling is part diary, part therapy, and part planning. Founders are inclined to bottle things up and to extenuate the loneliness they are naturally going to experience. Journaling helps to overcome this by being an outlet for Founders' thoughts, fears, and ambitions. The act of journaling frees the Founder's mind and is a cleansing exercise. Journaling gets things out of the Founder's mind and opens up space for new things and for creativity. A cluttered and bottled up mind becomes increasingly unproductive for Founders. Journaling is a way for Founders to cleanse and document; it also serves as a platform for thoughts and ideas to take root and grow. The ability for Founders to capture what they're thinking, feeling, and experiencing is the best way to identify areas for improvement and areas of opportunity. A journal also provides a breadcrumb trail of thoughts to allow a Founder to see how their perspective around something has evolved over time. This is important because Founders often lose sight of how and why they think and feel differently about something than they did previously. A journal is a mind map of the Founder's journey and forces a Founder to slow down long enough to contemplate, helping to bring order for the Founder daily.

## No Regrets

Bringing order to their lives helps Founders to have no regrets. Companies fail. Often. Companies redirect constantly. Founders are flawed. Founders will make constant, countless mistakes. Founders make it all personal and take it all personally. It would be foolish to suggest otherwise. It is healthier and more productive for Founders to acknowledge they are not the business and the business doesn't define them as a person, but being a Founder is a very personal endeavor. I've not been very good at separating myself from the success or failure of companies; others are probably much better at this than I am. One of things I have been good at, even while taking the outcome personally, is not having regrets. Regrets mean you didn't act and decide properly based on the information you had at the time. If you are making what you believe is the best decision at a moment in time based on the information you have at that time then you shouldn't have any regrets. Regrets come from when we knowingly make a decision in opposition to the information we have. For Founders, having order in their lives helps them with decision making that removes regrets. Of course wrong decisions will be made, but move on from them without regret. Making mistakes doesn't mean you have to and should live with regret forever. As long as you made the best decision you could at the time, irrespective of the outcome, you can live without regrets.

## Clutter

When I see a Founder surrounded by a lot of clutter and disorganization I become concerned. Clutter creates chaos and saps time and energy. If I go to a Founder's or startup's office and it's messy and cluttered, I immediately start to question the Founder's ability to execute well over a long period. I've seen the studies and articles that say a messy desk and space can be associated with intelligence and creativity. That might be true, but experience tells me that Founders who surrounds themselves with clutter and noise, are not bringing order to areas that he or she can easily bring order to and therefore are making things even harder than they need to be. By allowing clutter to exist around them, Founders create consequential dynamics, even though they may not realize it. Founders who are accustomed to clutter usually have worse pitch decks, give ineffective pitches and presentations, and don't communicate with brevity and candor. Living with clutter infests and impacts every aspect of a Founder's life and work. If I see a Founder's desktop and it is littered with files, I'm concerned about their ability to organize and prioritize. It is a small thing that is representative of a larger problem. Founders should de-clutter and simplify. Founders who are minimalists and who operate with the objective of minimalism in their personal and professional lives have the space and energy to think more clearly and to operate more efficiently than those who are bogged down with inconsequential stuff.

## Thrashing

Thrashing will kill a Founder and a company. Thrashing comes from a lack of order. One of the challenges for first responders and people like lifeguards is dealing with someone who is thrashing. The thrashing makes it hard for them to help the person because of the unpredictability, time, and energy that is consumed as part of the thrashing. The same happens for Founders and startups that are thrashing. Time and energy get sucked up and used by the thrashing, and the unpredictability creates an unproductive and confusing environment. Too much thrashing, for too long, can also become the culture of the startup and the standard operating mode for a Founder. If this happens the Founder and company are likely doomed; they just haven't realized it yet. Thrashing fills the void left by a lack of order. In the absence of order chaos and thrashing take place.

Earlier in my career, I used to thrash a lot. Motion and busyness seemed to be what was called for, so I did it. All of it. I ran around, frenetically trying to get a lot done. It took me time to realize that it was unproductive and not producing the results I wanted for myself, for the rest of the team, and the company. Doing a lot isn't as important as doing the right things well. Quality over quantity is imperative for Founders and this is a hard balance to strike and lesson to learn because there is already too much to be done. But scrambling to get a lot done, being unfocused, and sapping all of your energy in the process isn't the answer that many Founders think it is. It just means you haven't figured out what the most important things are at any point in time and you are thrashing as a result.

## Structure

Founders need structure for themselves, for the team, and the company overall. I'm not talking about organizational charts and hierarchies most often associated with a company structure. Quite the opposite in fact. I think startups should remain as flat as they can for as long as they can. Being flat democratizes roles and contributions and prevents organizational bloat and politics around ladder climbing and things such as titles. Flat focuses on the work and on progress. The structure I am referencing is structure that provides for efficiencies and productivity. Structure around how meetings will be conducted, how collaboration will occur (both internally and externally), how communication will happen. Most people have now heard of Amazon's two pizza rule. The essence is if it takes more than two pizzas to feed a team, the team is too big. This is structure. I've come to believe that every interaction between people should have a purpose. Why is the meeting or call happening? What decisions need to be made? Who is making them? What is everyone's role? Are some people there for context and to offer information as needed to help with the decision or do they have a voice in the decision? Meetings are generally disliked because they lack focus, intent, and structure. Meetings that are decision focused will provide much more value and allow a startup to make decisions much faster. You would think that startups wouldn't have structure challenges, especially early on when the team is small, but they do and if allowed to continue these will become part of the company's normal operating mode. Just as it is easy for startups to begin to drift away from customers, without even realizing it's happening, startups can also begin to get loose with structure easily. It doesn't take long for a startup that is adding team members at a fast pace to begin to have unfocused and unproductive meetings. Founders need to determine how they want to bring structure to how the company interacts internally and externally. This structure helps bring order and is also a major contributing factor to the company's culture.

## CHAPTER 15
# Run to the Fire

The essence of being a Founder is being a problem solver. This means running to problems, not away from them. I describe this as running to the fire because we're not wired to seek out and run to problems, repeatedly. The existence of a Founder is a never-ending cycle of problems and challenges and the tendency is for Founders to fatigue and run away from problems over time. To be a successful Founder you have to run to the fire.

## Confrontation

Founders have to get comfortable with confrontation. Confrontation is a natural part of the stream of problems to solve. Founders who avoid confrontation are accumulating problems and decision debt. Eventually, the accumulated decision debt becomes unwieldy and insurmountable. Founders should not seek out disagreements and confrontations, but they also should not be surprised when they occur and should deal with them head on. I recently came across a startup that was licensing the core of their product from another startup, a failed startup at that. The Founders acknowledged they were having a difficult time getting the product aligned to what the business needed and the other company was moving too slowly. Oh yeah, the kicker here is the other startup was still doing the development on the product as part of the arrangement. The arrangement was clearly one-sided and was not working for the startup that thought it was getting a leg up by licensing the product. I asked the Founder of the licensing startup if they had confronted the licensee with the issues and the fact that the arrangement was not working well enough under its current structure to keep doing it. The Founder said he hadn't yet but was planning on it. I asked how long this had been a known problem and he said for several months, since the beginning of the arrangement. And yet, he hadn't done anything about it. Confrontation and problem avoidance has always been and will always be a failed approach for Founders. Whereas a strategic decision to delay a negotiation until the Founder feels they are in a better negotiation position can be wise, avoiding confrontation is almost never a good idea. Founders who avoid confrontation will one day realize they have a mountain of unresolved problems confronting them that is now potentially crippling both personally and for the company. Problems, especially ones of consequence, do not magically go away.

One reason Founders avoid confrontation is because they are unsure if they have the right answer so they will avoid confrontation hoping the right answer will come to them eventually. Founders also want to be liked, as we all do, so they will avoid confrontation so as to not create a situation where someone will dislike them. Founders mistakingly believe that everyone needs to like them in order to create a successful company. This comes from a Founder's lack of confidence, loneliness, and feelings of imposter syndrome.

Because Founders are often starting with nothing more than a problem hypothesis and the belief they can solve the problem, they believe they are in a weak position to ruffle feathers and to stand their ground. The opposite is actually true. I'm not saying Founders should be assholes but they also shouldn't be pushovers. Working in the best interest of the company sometimes means you won't be liked by everyone and you have to make hard choices that you have to live with.

## Advisors and service providers

Founders can get more comfortable solving problems and running toward them instead of away if they have a team of experienced and trusted advisors backing them up. This is not easy to develop and put in place, but it is worth the time and effort. Founders will be approached by many advisors, vendors, and service providers. Founders need to vet all of them with great care and they should interview and consider several before making a decision about who to engage with. The right team of advisors for a Founder is one of the single biggest decisions he or she will make. A Founder who has exceptional, experienced advisors is emboldened to believe they can take on any problem that develops. And they're right. A great attorney who understands startups and the journey a startup goes through is invaluable. Same with a financial advisor and operational advisor. Investors can be included in this mix, but a word of caution around investors providing advice. Investors have a fiduciary responsibility to their Limited Partners (LPs) to provide them a return on their money. This responsibility supersedes their responsibility to you. Attorneys and accountants hold themselves responsible and they have accreditation bodies that also expect them to act in your best interest. The best ones don't need the governing bodies to do so. They know the importance of their work and guidance and they act accordingly.

    The best way to find advisors with the startup experience and expertise you need is to observe and ask. Don't just look for the loudest and busiest. Look for and find out who is doing the most consequential work with startups that are having the most success. In fact, the advisors and vendors that run around with the loudest bullhorn and who spew nonsense are typically the ones you don't want to work with and should avoid. There is a reason they have to create so much noise and spew garbage. They aren't and haven't been part of anything of substance and to any degree of success, so they create a lot of noise to garner attention. The best advisors and service providers get to work accomplishing for their clients. Yes, they are visible and present, but in a valuable, respectful way. They are likely the ones conducting workshops, sponsoring events, and providing real value to the startup community. They are additive to the startup community they are in and they often put more in than they ever get out. New Founders that don't have the network and relationships can ask more experienced, successful Founders for referrals to advisors and service providers who have run to the fire with them. Experienced Founders typically know who to avoid and who to have as part of the team. New Founders should tap into and use the experience and relationships of experienced Founders. Experienced Founders are happy to make recommendations and introductions to help new Founders. Getting a referral from an experienced

Founder to advisors and service providers that know what it's like to run to the fire with the Founder, is advice that every Founder should seek. I know many excellent advisors and service providers, if you are seeking someone to run to the fire with, send me a message and I will be happy to make an introduction.

## Leading by example

If you want to build a culture of problem solving and accountability your team needs to see you running to the fire. I've seen many Founders who, because they are the Founder, expect to send team members running to the fire to solve problems, while the Founder avoids the problem altogether or sits back waiting for the problem to be solved. No one wants to follow someone who isn't willing to be first in line running to the fire, but everyone wants to follow and fight for someone who leads by confronting and solving tough problems. Being a leader is less about barking orders than it is about acting in a manner you want the team to act. Founders who run to the fire, are decisive, and those who hold themselves accountable will manifest similar behavior in the team. A lack of responsibility and accountability in a startup is toxic and creates a destructive environment of finger pointing and negativity that can kill a company. It's the Founders responsibility to set the example and tone for the rest of the team to follow. If the team knows the Founder will run to the fire whenever needed, they will too. The team will also be empowered to run to the fire and to begin to solve problems on their own without needing to get the Founder involved. When a startup gets to the point of having a culture in which everyone is expected to and is empowered to run to the fire, the team has an important ingredient to becoming high-performing. Founders shouldn't have to and can't solve every problem the company has to deal with so Founders need to create a culture of problem solving that is ever present. Once the team knows the Founder will run to the fire, they will too, and they will eventually do it on their own allowing the company to grow and thrive as a result.

## Courage

Founders have to be courageous and they have to instill it in the team. Starting and running a company takes courage. Running to the fire and confronting problems head-on takes courage. Courage and fear, well fearlessness, often get confused. Courage isn't the absence of fear; it is acting in the face of fear. Founders have to demonstrate courage if they expect the team to be courageous and to take on challenges that at the outset seem insurmountable. Most people, let alone Founders, are not naturally courageous. It is a skill learned over time and through experiences that provide a feedback loop of progress and satisfaction. Being courageous doesn't always need to be a life-threatening situation either. Someone who is afraid to speak in public but who overcomes the fear to do it because it is what the company needs is acting courageously. When a Founder or team member acts courageously it needs to be acknowledged and celebrated immediately. The recognition that they acted in the face of fear is critical to encouraging a culture of courage in which everyone feels supported and safe when they do something that scares them. Fear is always present. Being fearless isn't the objective, but being courageous is.

## Tools

An important part of running to the fire is having the tools to be able to deal with the problem when you get there. The best problem solvers know what tools they have at their disposal and how to use them expertly. In a startup some of the tools will vary by team member and role. An engineer will use a different set of tools to help solve a problem than the marketing person will. The Founder needs to empower team members with the right tools and team members need to make it known what tools they need. Running toward a fire without knowing what you can do when you get there and how you are going to do it wastes precious time and energy.

## Context

Founders and the team need to have as much data about the problem as possible. It will never be a complete set of data, but they will need to be able to believe in and trust what is available. How did the problem start? When did we first know about it? How did we find out? Who first encountered it? What's been tried so far, if anything? By whom and what were the results? Is the problem getting worse or is it contained? Who does it affect and to what degree? What are the options that have been evaluated? What if we do nothing? These and more are some of the context Founders and the team need to be able to assess and act swiftly on problems. Founders and startup teams that get good at problem diagnosis and context improve their odds of making good decisions, quickly.

# Startup Flow

## CHAPTER 16
# Introduction

As I have already mentioned, starting a company is an irrational act. The odds are stacked against every company surviving, let alone being successful. In some ways this is good and is as it should be. It isn't easy to solve a problem that customers care about enough to pay for your solution, so only the companies that are successful, earn it.

The idea of earning everything you accomplish as a company is an important perspective. No company, yes even yours, deserves anything. Companies don't deserve to solve a problem, or have customers, or to have investors. Companies earn it. The team earns it. Every bit of it. I see many companies acting as though they are deserving of success because they are trying and well-intended. It doesn't work that way of course, but many startups have the wrong perspective.

This section highlights some of the areas startups need to be aware of and get right to earn success, including:
- Being investable
- Timing
- Constraints
- Accelerators
- Sales
- Product Management
- Funding through customers

The principles for starting and building a successful company I reference are important and in some cases misunderstood or not understood at all. In my experience these are the principles needed for a startup to increase its odds of success.

CHAPTER 17

# Niche First

One result of understanding a problem at an expert level is that initially you might be solving a niche problem in a niche market, and that's okay. Solving a high-value problem for a few is more important than solving a low-value problem for many. The high-value problem for the few can evolve into solving it for many over time and maybe with some twists and turns. Solving a low-value problem for many has nowhere to go. It's dead and unsustainable. You just haven't admitted it.

I see many startups focused on scale. Scale doesn't matter until you are solving a high-value problem in a way a few customers care about. Getting ready for and anticipating scale seems to be a bit of a high for startups. Talking about and preparing for scale makes us feel like we are going to make it and in a big way. No small-time thinking here. Only big will do, thanks. The problem with focusing on being consumed by scale prematurely is the scale will never actually happen because of it. Getting things like this out of order gets punished. Scale too early and you won't even have 10 customers, let alone 100, or 1,000, or 10,000. You can prepare to scale when the time is right. In fact, it has never been easier to scale, at least from a product perspective. The days of product scaling being incredibly hard and expensive are mostly gone. The focus now needs to be on solving a high-value problem in a high-value way. The product can scale. The company can too if you nail the Customer-Product Fit.

Another reason to start with a niche and not be concerned with scale early is you will learn a ton about the problem and customers while you are narrow and focused. The value of creating something 10 people love and use with devotion is a major sign you have the potential to solve the same problem or a similar problem for many more. We get so caught up in scale and the hype around scale that we often discount and ignore the opportunity to solve a high-value problem for a small, niche group of customers that then has the potential of being a kernel for scale. Stay attuned to and don't turn away from niche problems. Here are some examples of companies and products that started very niche, but stayed close to customers and ended up scaling beyond anyone's initial expectations of what was possible:

- Airbnb: Began as an app to rent air mattresses on floors mostly for people who didn't have the money to spend on expensive hotel rooms.
- Facebook: Started out as "hot or not?" from a Harvard dorm room. Turns out people wanted a new way to be digitally connected.
- Ebay: An online trading platform for Pez dispensers that now allows peer-to-peer selling of anything.

## CHAPTER 18
# Manage to Pro Forma

If you've received investment you have a pro forma. If you haven't received an investment and are funding through customers you should still have one. The pro forma becomes your GPS for the company. Are you on track or off track? When, by how much, and why? If you don't have a pro forma or don't manage to the one you have, you can't accurately track the company performance. If you can't track the company's performance you are the captain of a ship with no rudder, adrift.

Everyone is expecting you are managing the company by the pro forma. Investors, the team, and customers expect you to have a good handle on the performance of the company. Your management of the pro forma is a key aspect of you evolving from being a Founder to being a company operator. In fact, when I am discussing Founders with other investors, one of the things I discuss with them is whether the Founder is a good operator. Managing to the pro forma and evolving as the company evolves is what makes a Founder a good operator. Don't concern yourself with being a Founder. Don't focus on the label and what you think the implications are. Focus instead on being a problem solver and a great operator. Founders that don't make this shift don't succeed, their companies don't succeed, or at least the company doesn't succeed with them leading it. This is one of the primary reasons Founders get replaced by professional, experienced operators as a company grows. The Founder never embraced being an operator, which starts with managing to a pro forma.

I was meeting with a client of my product consulting firm recently and he told me his lead investor thanked him for managing to the pro forma because most of their Founders don't. Investors will expect Founders to manage to the pro forma and will chastise them for not doing it, but investors don't sign up to babysit Founders. Because our client manages to his pro forma his investors like and trust him. His investors, especially his lead investor, has led multiple rounds of investment, has recruited other investors, and fights for the Founder and company.

Founders make a lot of excuses when they aren't managing to the pro forma. There is too much going on so they're too busy. There are more important things. The company is moving too fast and changing too much to be able to create and update an accurate pro forma. Yes, excuses and nonsense. Everything matters for startups and for Founders, but everything doesn't matter equally at any given point in time and certainly not continually. Having and managing to a pro forma is one of the things that matters all the time for Founders. Prove you are not just a Founder, which is a label anyone can give themselves, but prove you are a great operator by managing to a pro forma.

A pro forma can be adjusted and modified as warranted by the needs of the company and the dynamics of changing circumstances, but this doesn't give Founders license to view a pro forma as irrelevant or unimportant. The opposite is true. The faster a company is changing the more important it is to have a pro forma and to be managing to it. Not managing to a pro forma means Founders are winging it. Obviously not ideal. The client I referenced above has a very complex product and company that is changing and shifting constantly. You know how he handles it? He manages to the pro forma and when changes need to be made to reflect the new and future state of the company he communicates accordingly with the board, investors, partners, and the team, then adjusts the pro forma based on the new information.

Founders attempting to navigate the direction of the company without a pro forma are guessing and making uninformed decisions. Founders working in the best interest of the company and the key stakeholders take being a great operator seriously and managing to a pro forma is an important aspect of being a great operator.

CHAPTER 19

# Fail Fast is BS

I'm not a fan of clichés that develop around starting a company. Fail fast is one of my least favorites. I get the origin and essence, but just rattling off fail fast as advice to a startup team is lame and lazy. I've seen it be referenced and misused by many startup teams.

The meaning of fail fast is to move at a fast pace and if you end up going over a cliff around some aspect of the product or company, then you use that as a learning experience and restart. The problem with this narrative is that too many startups then use failing as some sort of an accomplishment and badge of honor. It's not. I've been there. It just means you failed. In my experience, most startups don't have the runway of time or money to fail. Quickly or slowly. Fail fast creates a mentality, even when there are signs things aren't working, to keep heading fast in the same direction, hoping things will somehow get better before the cliff appears.

Yes, startups need to move uncomfortably fast, but while learning and iterating with customers about the problem and the product. The intent is to understand the problem deeply and to create a solution customers value and will pay for, not to just crank out whatever you can quickly and easily.

Fail fast became part of the startup lexicon during a time when startup teams were still seeking solutions and building without extensive problem understanding and without getting close to customers about the problem and potential solutions. Fail fast made it okay to ignore these important principles and made it okay for startups to build recklessly. If startups adopt the fail fast mentality now, given the more evolved and informed principles and process to build successful products and companies, they will indeed fail.

**CHAPTER 20**

# Service to Product

Many startups initially are service firms. This is sometimes strategic as the company builds the early product and sometimes it is of necessity to generate cash. In either case, it can be beneficial to start out providing services, but with caution and awareness.

Service firms and product companies have very different business models. Service firms sell expertise and the experience of the team. This really means selling time. Whether a service firm charges by the hour, fixed fee by project, or some hybrid, ultimately the firm is selling the production time of the team. Service firms are hard to scale and grow because the product is really the team, and growing the team to be able to produce more work comes with numerous complications. Product companies build a product and then charge for the use of the product over time in some manner. Product companies can scale, where service firms can't. This is also why most investable companies are product companies and not service firms. Service firms don't produce enough profit margin along with limited scale, making them poor return-on-investment vehicles for investors.

Most startups that start out providing services with the intention of creating a product can't make the transition from services to product. The startup puts too much emphasis and focus on providing the service and not enough on the product. The startup also becomes dependent on the cash generated from the services. The startup grows the team to support providing the service, which then creates a cash flow challenge that only gets addressed, temporarily, by doing more of the servicing. Startups that get too deeply into providing services usually can't make the transition back to being a product company.

Startups can make providing services initially work to their advantage and to make the transition to being a product company easier by using the initial servicing period as a way to understand the problem better and to get close to customers. The cash from the services isn't nearly as important as the learning and relationship building. It becomes more like service clients paying the startup to get better informed so the service clients will become product customers. The goal is to be a product company that also might provide professional services to customers versus a services firm that has a half-baked product that customers won't use and pay for.

I've been through this. In one case we were a services firm first with no real product intention that identified a problem a product could solve and began to make the shift from being a services firm to a product company. During the shift we realized the services company could still continue as is and we established a new company and brand for the product company. This was made easier because the services firm and product company sold to the same industry and customers. The fact that we were providing services to clients that would become product customers helped make the product undeniably valuable from the first version.

Leverage providing services to clients to build a better product and to become a better product company. However, don't get hooked on and fall in love with being a service firm or you will likely never get away from it.

CHAPTER 21
# Be investable

John Huston is the former leader of Ohio Tech Angel Fund (OTAF). As you can probably guess, OTAF is a group of angel investors. One of things John would lament about often is how many startups put the responsibility of investing on the investors instead of coming to terms with and owning the startup's invest-ability. I've had several conversations with John and also heard him tell startups that instead of bashing investors, become investable, or realize your company is never going to be an investable one.

So what does it mean to be investable? In the simplest terms venture investors are looking for a high rate of return in a short time frame. To get venture investment, startups need to be able to paint a picture that demonstrates a viable and believable path to get to a size (value, really), fast enough that venture investors see more return than risk.

Digging a little deeper, being investable includes most of the principles referenced in this book. You have to be solving a high-value problem, demonstrate your knowledge of the problem, validate your ability to execute, and confirm you have the team committed and capable of dealing with the ups and downs of growing a company. Investors will also want to know how you will use the money. Investors want to know because they are assessing how well you know the state of the business and where the money can be best put to use and leveraged. Before seeking investment you need to know how you will use it and be able to convey that effectively to investors. I've seen many investment pitches go sideways because the startup could not clearly articulate how it was going to use the investment. Investors won't write checks if a startup can't tell them how the money will be used.

Unfortunately I still see a lot of startups pursuing venture investment when they are not investable and then blaming the investor community. Startups need to understand what it means and takes to be investable and if they aren't, then to decide whether they ever can be investable and take the steps to get there. Pursuing venture investment when a startup is not investable is a waste of time and energy for everyone, but mostly for the startup. Investors have time on their side, startups don't. A startup wasting time trying to persuade investors to invest when the startup is not investable harms the startup more than it does investors.

Startups also need to realize that investors don't have an obligation to tell you why they're not interested and not investing. The good ones do provide that feedback, but no investor is obligated to provide an explanation for their decision. Instead, startups should have the objective and put in the work to be undeniable to investors. If a startup gets to the point of being undeniable, the startup will have no issues raising investment. In fact, the startup will likely have multiple investors pursuing it.

It's also worth noting that if you are investable and receive investment, it's validation that you are able to convince an investor to invest but don't extrapolate it into more than that. Receiving investment is a single act and transaction in a series of countless acts and transactions. If you receive investment don't look at it as a finish line or an accomplishment that means more than it does. I've seen too many promising startups receive investment and then lose focus and take their foot off the gas. The opposite should actually happen. Receiving investment is fuel. Squandering fuel in any expedition, and make no mistake starting a company is an expedition, is irresponsible. Receiving investment is not the objective. Investment is there to drive other objectives, not an objective unto itself. Receiving investment is an important transaction, one you should be proud of, but investment doesn't make a great product, doesn't mean you understand the problem at an expert level, and doesn't mean you know how to tell a compelling story around any of it.

I'm not a huge fan of pitch competitions where prize money is awarded. Too often the winning of a pitch competition and a small amount of money establishes the wrong mindset for the startup. Winning a pitch competition doesn't make the company investable. Startups that win $5,000–$20,000 at a pitch competition often think it will now be easier for them to get investment. It won't be. Investors, from angels up to larger VC firms, don't care if a startup won a pitch competition. The investors will care about the things they always care about—team capability, problem understanding, problem value, and product-customer fit. Investors are approached by startups who have participated in and won pitch competitions all the time. This is not a differentiator for a startup. Sound fundamentals are a differentiator as investors see far fewer companies with sound fundamentals than those that have won pitch competitions. Winning a pitch competition doesn't make a startup investable.

Many investors and venture capital firms will not invest in single Founders. Single Founders are viewed as riskier than investing in Founding teams. It makes sense to a degree. Venture investing is about risk mitigation and one of the ways to mitigate risk is to invest in a team rather than an individual. Being single threaded through a single Founder is a major risk for investors. Everything from the Founder dying, to a spouse wanting to relocate, to the Founder just doing a bad job, and countless other reasons make it a risky proposition. Investors also question a single Founder's ability to recruit a team, sell, and otherwise attract the necessary people and organizations to engage with the company if they can't find Co-Founders.

I don't disagree with the risk associated to single-Founder companies, but I've seen some investors take it to the extreme. I've seen well informed, capable, and committed Founders spend so much time recruiting other Founders to help start the company that they lose too much time and become fatigued in the process so that the company never gets off the ground. Maybe this is the just outcome and the investor's perspective gets validated. But maybe sole Founders have the knowledge and capability to make it work on their own and fabulously. If you are a sole Founder understand the perspective investors might have about it and be prepared to deal with them before you encounter them. I would also suggest that you focus more on the problem, customers, and being the best Founder you can be versus becoming consumed with finding Co-Founders. If you focus on the most important things, the investors will come because you will have proven your ability to understand and solve a high-value problem customers care about and will pay for.

When seeking investment at varying stages of a company's evolution, startups need to know what investors are looking for at that stage. The attributes of being investable change as a startup evolves and grows. Telling the same story when raising a seed round that was being told when raising angel funding won't work and so on. Being investable means a startup has to evolve to be investable in different ways at different times. When startups struggle to move up the investment ladder, it is often a sign that the startup didn't know what the attributes of being investable at different stages meant and looked like. Of course, not being able to raise additional, larger investment can also be a sign a startup has not executed well enough to warrant being investable from a larger investment perspective. Being investable is an evolution and is in direct relation to a startup's evolution.

## CHAPTER 22
# Timing

Timing is crucial in starting a company. Assessing whether the timing is right is more art than science, but getting the timing right or wrong can be the difference between the company succeeding or failing.

One important reason to get and stay close to customers is that the interactions with and learnings from customers is the best and surest way to assess timing. If customers aren't ready or capable of buying, you might be too early. If customers don't value what you are doing, you might be too late or just missing the mark. Too early or too late are both incredibly difficult to overcome and most startups that are off on timing won't be able to overcome it. If a startup is too early it will need an a long runway of time, patience, and money. All three are in short supply these days (really always). Being too late likely means the window of opportunity to create a product and company that customers value is closed or so small it may not be an opportunity worth pursuing. Opportunities with very small windows mean your margin will be lower and your costs higher as you will be in a fight to get customers' attention and will likely have to compete on price.

During a workshop I was running at a corporate innovation conference, a guy stood up and said that visionaries like Steve Jobs, Elon Musk, and Jeff Bezos don't care about and pay attention to timing; they have a vision and they move forward in pursuit of the vision, regardless of anything else. Even if this is true, although I don't believe it is, why take the chance of the timing being off? This is about increasing odds and leveraging fundamental principles to do so. Timing and the circumstances being right to start a company is a critical piece of the mix. In all references the guy brought up, the circumstances facilitated and allowed visions to become reality and to succeed. Apple, Tesla, and Amazon have certainly innovated along the way and created value by extending and evolving technologies, processes, and systems where others hadn't, but the underpinnings were there for them to leverage.

Bill Gross (Founder of Idealab) was the first person I remember highlighting the importance of timing in startup success. In his 2015 TED Talk he speaks of how he discovered that timing was a more significant factor to a company's success than any other single factor. In fact he discovered it was more significant than several other factors put together. His research uncovered timing was a significant factor 42 percent of the time. I've paid more attention to the role timing plays in starting a company ever since, and I agree with Bill. Not sure about the precise percentages he came up with, but overall, timing is a critical factor that cannot be overlooked.

Timing presents a challenge for Founders, startup teams, and investors.

**Founders** want to go at the problem and company hard, now. Once a Founder gets the itch to solve a problem and to start a company to solve it, they have to scratch the itch. However Founders need to be able to step back during the early days of problem understanding and customer validation to realistically assess whether the timing is right. Occasionally, but rarely, Founders can change the dynamics of timing with some shrewd moves and storytelling. Most often the timing is either right or wrong.

**Startup team members** need to be able to assess the timing to determine what company they want to join first of all and, if they have joined a team, what the timing implications are for the product, and marketing and selling it.

**Investors** evaluate timing from their first exposure to the company, product, and space/problem. If the timing is right, the investors capital will be more actionable and put to better use. If the timing is wrong, they know the company will have to raise more from them and likely others to extend the company's runway to wait for the right time. A badly timed startup, irrespective of everything else being stellar, is a bad investment.

Starting a company at the wrong time requires a herculean effort to overcome. And most of the time it doesn't work. Startups need to honestly assess the environment, circumstances, and timing of starting the company. If a startup has regulatory, customer behavior, market factors, economic conditions, technical limitations, or myriad other things creating head wind, the startup needs to take an honest look at whether the negative factors can be overcome with a reasonable amount of effort, time, and money.

CHAPTER 23
# Constraints

One reason large companies are not as good at creating new products and get out innovated by startups is because large companies have too much. Too much of everything. Too much money, too many people, too many systems, too much.

Startups succeed in creating new, disruptive products where large companies fail in part because of constraints, not in spite of them. Constraints are good. Constraints force focus, agility, urgency, thriftiness, humility, curiosity, and more. The challenge for startup teams is believing this and embracing it, instead of bemoaning scarcity.

You might be thinking there is a limit to the benefit of constraints if a startup remains over constrained for too long and you would be right. Most startups have a finite amount of time, money, and energy to execute to a level where continued investment of any of these things and more makes sense. A resource-starved startup will eventually succumb to the scarcity. I'm making the case that overabundance is a worse situation when creating new, disruptive products and companies on top of the products than being constrained, and that actually, a short-term state of constraints is beneficial.

## Focus & discipline
Constraints drive focus from a lack of extraneous compli-

cation. When you can operate in an environment free of bureaucracy, politics, and career positioning you can focus on what matters right now. Abundance creates options. Options when starting a company can create an unfocused and undisciplined environment. There has been a lot of discussion and debate of whether a startup should have a Plan A, Plan B, and maybe even a Plan C. While it can be beneficial to map out likely scenarios and variables so a startup isn't completely caught off guard by having to redirect (ugh, pivot), working more than one plan at a time is unfocused and undisciplined. Constraints force fewer options which helps us focus on working a plan, which is the best, most likely plan to produce the outcomes we want.

## Customer centricity

Large company have a fair amount of customers that equate to the size of the company. You would think this abundance of customers would be an advantage for large companies when creating new products. It isn't. It is a disadvantage in most cases, because large companies operate in fear of losing their bevy of customers and the fact they have a lot of customers inflates their egos to the point they aren't close to their customers. Large company customers become funnels, channels, and queues. Large companies have even gotten to the point of representing the voice of their customers through an approach called, "Voice of Customer," where the customer gets acknowledged from a distance rather than having a continuous seat at the table. Startups don't have any customers at the beginning so this forces them to initially get and stay close to customers.

## Prioritization

Constraints make it easier to prioritize the many things that need to be done. This is counter-intuitive because having more resources appears to create an environment where more can get done while seemingly also making it easier to prioritize. The opposite is most often true. Constraints force ruthless prioritization because the time, resources, and money are not present to be able to take on a bunch of things at the same time. Prioritizing is challenging for most people. We want to be sure we're making the right decision. We desire and seek certainty and often in some of the most uncertain circumstances. The more uncertain the circumstances, the more we desire certainty. Sometimes we can't even focus on anything else. We become consumed with finding certainty. This conflict between needing certainty inside of a highly uncertain situation is acute in a startup. That's where the value of the constraints comes in. The constraints reduce the number of viable options to a more manageable list. It's still not easy to overcome the feelings and emotions, but constraints are powerful in removing complication.

## Speed

Constraints help you move faster in all areas of the company, not just product. Constraints help to establish a speed of culture, work, and decision making. The value of time increases in direct proportion to the runway available. The shorter the runway for a startup the more likely it is to move swiftly and to make decisions quickly. Runway is most often associated to funding and that probably makes sense because more money allows a startup to hire more, market more, and make more mistakes. However, runway also includes things like customer attention span and interest. If it takes you too long to deliver something of value to customers or if you have to redirect (pivot as it is commonly referred to in startup jargon) too many times, customer interest and attention will wane. Scarcity of resources for startups causes them to act with a greater sense of urgency, even if the startup doesn't want to or is uncomfortable operating with urgency. The constraints leave no choice and that's good.

## Camaraderie

Constraints drive startup teams to work together in an us against the world way. I've rarely seen this inside a corporation. In fact, if anything, you see the exact opposite. People on a corporate team supposedly are working to the same end, when in reality, they often are working to different ends and likely personally selfish ones. Abundance doesn't galvanize people the way constraints do. Constraints build bonds between people. A shared struggle most commonly exists in situations with immense constraints. A shared struggle brings us together in a real and authentic way. Corporations try to recreate the struggle by forming small project teams with unrealistic timeframes, and fixed budgets. It rarely works. It doesn't work because corporations can't replicate the underlying realities of a startup. When a project at a corporation fails, the team moves on to various other projects. Sure, with a bad taste in their mouths, but they move on. When things at a startup fail people don't get paid, investors lose money, and Founders go into debt, maybe go bankrupt.

Corporations have a safety net. Startups fall onto a bed of nails, all pointed up.

## Risk

Constraints help us deal with risk better. It's another reason corporations are less effective at creating new, disruptive products. When there is a lot on the line, a lot to lose, we become more risk adverse as people and organizations. This perspective shift around risk tolerance happens quickly, too. I've experienced it myself and I've seen startups start out fearless, then within only a few months and after a little bit of traction begin to get more conservative and protective. This is a natural reaction. At the outset of starting a company there is less to lose. Pride and ego are what's most at risk and once you get beyond that you realize you can live with the other consequences should it all go off the rails. As the company grows and there is more of everything to lose, it becomes harder to maintain the same level of daring. Constraints embolden us to operate more freely and fearlessly.

If you have a startup now, or start a company in the future, embrace and value the constraints as part of the process. Constraints are your friend and drive immense value that most of the time we are not aware of.

## CHAPTER 24
# Product Management

If there is one role and discipline in a startup that is now indispensable (probably always has been, we just didn't figure it out until recently) it is product management.

Product Management is the discipline of determining what matters most, at any moment in time to add value for customers and to accomplish the business outcomes for the company. You might recall my definition for a successful product from the introduction as, a product that solves a high-value problem customers care enough about to pay for it at a level that provides the business outcomes desired by the product owner. The role and discipline of Product Management is the single biggest factor in a startup creating a successful product. Product Management serves as the hub between customers and the startup's team of designers, developers, and business. One of the reasons startups create better, more innovative products than corporations with far more resources is because startups have embraced product management faster and better than their corporate counterparts.

You can't be good at innovation and creating new, disruptive products without being great at product management. Most large companies struggle with innovation because they aren't even good at product, let alone great. Innovation without being great at product means companies are merely doing an exercise in ideation. Let's see how many innovative ideas we can come up with and then feel satisfied with that because of the lack of product chops to actually convert the ideas into products. When I come across a large company struggling with innovation it isn't because it is lacking in resources. It's because it is lacking in know-how and process around product and more specifically product management.

In conversations with many startups and VC's the biggest talent shortage currently, and for the foreseeable future, isn't developers, it's product managers. Product Management is still a relatively new craft so there aren't a lot of experienced and capable Product Managers. Those that are, are likely in interesting roles, working on interesting products, at interesting companies making it hard for startups to lure them away. Startups in need of Product Management either need to be working on something more interesting than what an experienced product manager is currently working on or they need to hire inexperienced product managers and know there will be a ramp-up period to learn what product management is and what a product manager does. A startup can also engage with a product firm, like my firm AWH, to create early versions of the product while the startup builds out its internal team. We have done this many times, over the past few years, with startups in a variety of industries.

Without strong product management at a startup someone and something else is going to drive the product poorly and improperly. Here is what typically happens in the void:

*Sales drives the product.* This seems okay at first, but breaks down quickly and is difficult to overcome later. Once a startup has a sales-driven product culture and process, instilling a product person and product management discipline will be like giving the company a lobotomy. The company has likely had some success initially, which jades the perspective of leadership and the team to think they can just keep operating as they have. I know a dozen or so startups right now that fall into this category and there are hundreds, if not thousands more. What inevitably ends up happening is the company plateaus, the product stagnates, or the company ends up with several, very customized versions of the product which creates a variety of technical, operational, and scalability issues. Sales driven product management feels good, until it's a disaster that can't be overcome.

*Development drives the product.* Development determining what a product should do and how it should do it is akin to letting a drywall installer design a house. In the absence of product management at a startup this is often what happens. Too many startups see development as a necessity and product management as a nice to have. This is backwards. Not to say that development isn't important, it is of course, but great code can get written in many different ways. Great product management is at least an equal necessity to great development, if not superseding it. Development-driven products, similar to sales-driven products, might succeed for a short time, but as the product needs to evolve to remain relevant and valuable development-driven products end up having short lifespans.

If you're a startup that doesn't yet have a product discipline you need to be very intentional about getting it in place. It starts with the current team beginning to understand what a sound product discipline looks like and how it works. Getting a product discipline in place with the current team will also make it easier to hire a Product Manager and for the Product Manager to be able to plug in and add value faster. There is a lot of content available now on Product. Some resources to consider include: Mind The Product (mindtheproduct.com), Product Coalition (productcoalition.com), and Department of Product (departmentofproduct.com). Some of these organizations also put on conferences. There are also product management meetups happening in most cities now, as well as various workshops and other product centric events. The team at AWH has been fortunate to be part of helping to establish the product community in Columbus where the company is located. For example, in Columbus a Product Management workshop series launched that is being led and taught by experienced Product Managers. They're doing it to advance the craft and profession of product management. Columbus now also has a conference focused specifically on product called *Lift: Product Summit*. Lift has sold out every year so far.

So if you are a startup in need of product people, what should you do? First, get engaged in the local product community and activities. If there isn't a product community yet, then be part of starting it. Host product meetups at your offices, lead ProductTank (a part of Mind The Product), and begin to share product insights and valuable content with your community. Second, consider a remote product manager.

Since the product craft is still relatively new, it might take some time for your community to have knowledgeable and capable product people. You might have to look outside of your local area and consider adding product people who will work remotely.

Any startup that is gaining traction and growing at a fast pace is great at product. One can't happen without the other now. It's a primary differentiator between the startups that succeed and those that don't.

## CHAPTER 25
# Accelerators

Overall I'm not a huge fan of accelerators. Accelerators often serve as a crutch for too many startups and are viewed as some sort of finish line versus a starting line by many. Startups tout their inclusion in an accelerator like something major has been accomplished when what it really means is that the startup was more appealing than another set of startups at the same place and time, based on the pageant rules established by the accelerator. Acceptance and participation in an accelerator doesn't mean anything more than that.

Most successful startups don't go through an accelerator. History tells us the startups that have a committed, capable team that grinds everyday solving a high-value problem, in a way customers care about and will pay for, are the most successful. Is it because these startups don't participate in accelerators, probably not. It likely means they didn't need the services and support of an accelerator to succeed. On the other hand, many mediocre startups go through accelerators in hopes of evolving from their current mediocre state and most don't evolve enough to be successful. Sure startups will redirect and pivot as part of going through an accelerator, but it is rare that a startup goes in mediocre and comes out ready to take the world by storm.

Accelerator demo days are bad for startups. The challenge is that accelerators operate in cycles, classes, or cohorts. Pick your favorite time reference. The cycles have a demo day. The demo day is when the accelerator and the startups show off what they've been working on. However often it seems more like a pitch day for the accelerator rather than for the startups. Accelerators need their demo days to go well so they can keep investors and other supporters engaged and continue to operate. The demo day is an artificial point in time for startups and often startups get focused on building and having something slick for the demo day. They focus on finding solutions and building rather than on deep problem understanding and customer research and validation. So demo days come around. Startups pitch against enormous TAM (total addressable market) potential and do slick demos that have little customer alignment. Accelerator demo days force startups participating to solve and build rather than understand and validate.

Startups can get value out of an accelerator or incubator by being intentional and realistic about what the company needs that the accelerator can provide. The biggest value accelerators or incubators provide to a startup is typically a network of contacts for investment, team members, customers, and advisors. Far too often though the focus is on the advisors and not the other parties, which means startups just have more people in their ear providing opinions. Most startups don't need more advisors; they need fewer, more relevant advisors.

Startups should be aware of the value of accelerators and think realistically about whether the company needs to and should apply and participate or whether it just will be a distraction. Here is a brief self-assessment a startup can do to determine accelerator readiness, value, and fit.

- **Team**—How big, experienced, committed and capable is the team? Is the team just the Founder(s) or is it the Founders plus one or two other people? The larger and more experienced the team, the less likely a startup is to get value out of participating in an accelerator. If it is just the Founder(s), an accelerator might make more sense as it might be able to assist with recruiting more team members. Founder(s) will meet other people during the accelerator period who might want to jump on board versus continuing to pursue their own company.
- **Stage**—What stage is a startup in? Pre-product? Pre-revenue? V1 Product? Growth? Most accelerators are structured to work with early stage companies. Typically, pre-most things, except the Founders of course.
- **Product**—In large part because of the demo day referenced above most accelerators are focused on software companies. It's also because software product companies are the easiest to scale and increase margins as a result of the scaling. If a startup is not a software product company, accelerators likely won't make sense and taking the time to apply will be of no value. There is a sprinkling of hardware accelerators now, but they are few in number and not very mature. Even within software most accelerators are focused on very early products because that is what serves their business model best. Accelerators might be more effective and

valuable for startups if they have in the past worked with startups that have more evolved products, and if they focused more on helping the startups to improve the product and be more valuable to customers, rather than creating the product MVP (Minimal Viable Product).

- **Investment**—Most startups participate in an accelerator to get visibility with investors and to get to know them. This is a worthwhile goal and maybe it is the only way a startup will meet a particular investor, but I go back to the fact that most successful and venture-backed startups don't go through accelerators. So although a startup might meet some investors participating in an accelerator, the startup still has to be investable to make the introductions worthwhile and most startups going into and coming out of accelerators are not investable.

- **Network**—This is probably the single biggest reason for a startup to participate in an accelerator. The people you meet, especially the other Founders, are the real value. The ability to share experiences and insights with other Founders through an accelerator's alumni network can prove to be incredibly valuable. The relationships might not help you with the startup for which you join the accelerator, but over the long-term being able to tap into the learnings of the other Founders can be important.

- **Advisors**—Accelerators need to do a better job of vetting advisors and being more selective of the access they provide advisors to startups. I wrote a blog post a few years ago titled, "Beware The Leeches." I wrote it because of how many bad actors I saw in startup communities and accelerators across the country. Accelerators boast a large set of advisors because they believe it adds more credibility and is a recruiting tool to get more startups to engage with them. Accelerators would be better served and they would provide a better service to their startups by having a smaller, select set of advisors who are providing real value. Part of my concern is that bad advisors don't provide good advice, and their bad advice causes harm. I've seen many advisors who capitalize on a relationship with an accelerator for the advisor's sole benefit and with no regard to the veracity of help being provided to the startups.

- **Space**—In some cases, accelerators provide physical space for companies which is fine, but not necessary. The value of startups working in the same physical space together has been overblown and is really only valuable when the startups are working on tangential problems or industries. The physical proximity of startups for an accelerator is of more value to the accelerator than it is for the startups. The best performing accelerators don't care about their startups being co-located together or with the accelerator. Co-location of a startup with other non-tangential startups or an accelerator has no bearing on a startup's success. Accelerators that provide startups with funding through an accelerator's own fund often require startups receiving the funding to rent space in their facility. It is completely self-serving for the accelerator. On one hand, the accelerator is saying here is some funding with pretty onerous terms, and on the other, you have to pay us rent as a bonus. This double-dipping makes me crazy and is not working in the best interest of startups.

Y Combinator (YC) is probably the most well-known and successful accelerator. Although I still don't like many aspects of their model, including the demo day, I get why they do it. Outside of YC, accelerators overall have not proven to make that much of a difference for startups. Most accelerators popped up during a time when areas outside Silicon Valley were working to establish startup ecosystems and accelerators were deemed an important component to a successful startup ecosystem. I don't believe this was ever true and even if it were at one point, I don't think it is now. Brad Feld nailed it in his book, *Startup Communities*, where he says, "Entrepreneurs make and sustain a startup community." Accelerators don't make startups. Entrepreneurs and startups make accelerators.

## CHAPTER 26
# Sales

Outside of timing, the other most common reason I see for startups not succeeding is their inability to acquire customers. It's also one of the reasons to value Customer Product Fit over Market Product Fit. While a startup is establishing Customer Product Fit it is figuring out how to best position and sell the product. A startup has to figure out how to acquire customers effectively and efficiently. Although sales has transformed over the years and more is being done through various marketing strategies and inside of product, which is now known as Product Marketing, the ability to tell a compelling story and convert prospects into customers remains of critical importance. Sales proficiency is especially important with B2B companies and products.

Sales is storytelling. The best salespeople are the best storytellers. They understand the prospect's current situation and the pain associated with it. Then they create a vision of the prospect's new reality and the path to get there with their product or service. Defining and communicating the path to the new reality is paramount because the easiest thing for people to do is nothing. I strongly believe a Founder needs to be the company's first, best salesperson. The only way for the Founders to know how to build out the sales team and to hire the right sales team members is for them to know what it takes to sell for the company. Many high-potential products and companies die before they ever really get started, because no one on the founding team wanted to or was good at selling.

When I get into a discussion with a startup about sales and they haven't embraced and taken sales seriously, I suggest that one of the Founders get a sales trainer/coach. I value coaching more than training. Training is often a one-time thing that acts as a momentary shot of adrenaline, but isn't long lasting and often doesn't produce the desired results. However, coaching is ongoing, iterative, and evolutionary. Of course the ideal is ongoing training combined with ongoing coaching. In the absence of time, energy, and money, always pick coaching over training. A great coach will provide training during the coaching. Great trainers are not always great coaches. A great sales coach can progress an inexperienced Founder (and anyone else for that matter) into a reasonably effective salesperson pretty quickly. A person's innate personality and skills help to make the process go faster and to perform at a higher level. If a startup's team cannot decide among themselves who should lead sales and who should get sales coaching, they should engage a sales coach to do assessments of the team members to determine who is most likely to do well at sales based on their personalities and perspectives. The assessment process will also provide time to collaborate with some sales coaches to determine the best fit.

I see too many startups making critical errors around sales that end up never really giving the company a chance to succeed. These include:

- **Outsourcing sales**—A startup should never outsource

sales. First, I've rarely seen it work. Two, even on the rare occasion where I've seen it work, it isn't sustainable and ends up not working long-term. Why do startups outsource sales? Because the Founders didn't start the company to sell and be salespeople. They likely come from same other professional or educational background than sales. As a result, they don't understand sales as a business discipline and their lack of understanding creates ignorance around the importance, so they outsource it. Outsourcing lead generation can be highly effective and makes sense for some startups, but certainly not sales. And outsourcing lead generation can be a slippery slope for some startups because it can be a sign of apathy and de-valuing sales.

- **Partnerships**—Don't expect partnerships are going to do your selling for you. Distribution partnerships can be a great way to get to a broader market, faster for many startups. While a startup is likely new to a market and has little to no visibility or credibility, distribution partners often do. This is why distribution partners become very alluring to startups. Getting access to a partner's customers and network seems magical to a startup and seems to be a path to make that hockey stick growth chart a reality. Startups need to fight the allure and the quick fix promise of partnerships. Having a partner strategy is fine, but being too reliant on partners to drive sales is too risky. Remember, this is about increasing odds. Partnerships initially seem like they are odds increasers, but they almost never deliver to the level expected or needed. A better and more proven strategy

is to augment a startup's own sales efforts with those of partners, but with the startup's own sales efforts always being primary. A startup cannot be a good partner to a distribution partner without first being a good sales organization itself.
- **The product won't sell itself.** Irrespective of how smart and capable a startup's team is and how cutting-edge and advanced the product is, the belief that either is compelling enough for the product to sell itself is naive. Products don't sell themselves. In fact, when the problem being solved is more complex and sophisticated and requires specialization of the product, the startup likely will be selling to a highly knowledgeable and skeptical customer. Even fairly simplistic products need to be marketed and sold effectively. There is too much noise and too much friction.

A startup that understands and is competent at sales, combined with solid product management is an unstoppable force.

## CHAPTER 27
# Fund Through Customers

The best and the most overlooked source of funding for a startup is customers. Customer revenue of course, but also customers becoming investors in the product and company. The elusive traction that every startup is pursuing and investors are looking for is really validation that customers value and will pay for what a startup is doing and that the customers will increase their numbers over time. A startup's ability to generate, revenue and profit from operations, i.e. serving customers, is the most important step in validating that the startup is actually a business. Funding through customers has several advantages. Some of the advantages are obvious, while others are not. I've been a part of this happening and I've seen it work.

Customers buying your product can, in some cases, give you enough financial capacity to fund the growth of the company organically and to not need outside investment. Of course, this is the preferred method to fund a company. You don't have the distraction of having to raise outside investment. You don't have to give up any equity. You get important validations along the way that don't come as easily when funding doesn't come through operations and customers. Customer funding as part of their purchasing your product is often labeled as bootstrapping. My experience tells me bootstrapping and funding through customers purchasing are different enough to call it out. For me, bootstrapping is the Founders using scraped together funding from credit cards, personal loans, second mortgages, dipping into 401Ks, and the like to fund the company in-lieu of raising outside investment or because they've tried and can't. Bootstrapping also doesn't provide any business validation whereas customer funding through purchasing of the product means the company is already operating as a business and validating essential aspects of the business. Bootstrapping means self-funding. Funding through customers means so much more.

Customer funders can also be non-traditional outside investors where you get the best of customers seeing value in the product and being term and equity friendly investors. I've been part of a couple of situations where we got outside investment from customers and potential customers to build out the product and company. In all cases we didn't give up any equity. The customers received a royalty and special pricing considerations, but we didn't have to give up any equity. And the customers were fine with it. You need to know the motivations of customer funders and what they value to strike a mutually beneficial investment structure. In our cases, we knew the customers valued getting early access to the product, being able to help shape the product, being known as a leader and innovator in their space, and having a long-term royalty as an additional revenue stream for their companies. We were very aggressive with the terms of the royalty arrangements, to the customer's benefit. Structuring the royalties can be tricky, because you want the customer's participation to be valued throughout but not something you can't live with in the near and long term. In one case, a customer gave us a high six figure investment for an immediate and long-term royalty. The customer was the largest customer in the industry and I knew what it would mean to have them all in with us. So I made them an aggressive offer that valued their money as well as their expertise and other contributions. They received 80 percent of the margin until they recouped their investment and then 20 percent for the next five years. It's also important to note this was an enterprise product with a deal value of around $1 million, so we had the price point and margin to make this work and be lucrative for both. We were able to build the first version of the product, really up through version 3, with the customer funding and we never had to raise any further investment for the company. The fact that we didn't give up any equity as part of the customer funding came in very handy when the company eventually was sold.

Customer funders also help you build a better product as they can provide the subject matter expertise and problem context you otherwise don't have and that would take a long time to get. This point cannot be overstated. The ability to get and stay close to customers around the problem is crucial as identified below in *Chapter 38: Get and Stay Close to Customers*. Having an invested (literally) customer educating you and iterating with you on the problem and solutions is invaluable. Getting this intimate perspective and involvement is nearly impossible without an invested customer. An invested customer is not only working in your interest and the product's interest, but in theirs. This ownership position changes everything and accelerates your problem understanding, solution exactness, and customer product fit (Product Flow - Customer Product Fit) to a level you would never be able to achieve on your own.

Customer funders will also be market makers for you that are invaluable to your early business development efforts. You will be able to acquire other customers at lower cost than having to go to the market yourself, without the customer funder's help. A key to having the best customer funder(s) is for them to be respected and representative of the industry. In the case of the customer funder referenced above, they are the largest organization in the space, which meant I knew if we created a product with them that we would be creating a product anyone in the space could also use and value. This proved to be true beyond my initial expectations. What I hadn't thought about was that the customer funder had such a prominent position and voice in the space they could get on stage at all of the conferences and events for the space with little effort. We accompanied their team to the conferences and sometimes co-presented. Even when they presented solo, we were mentioned in the presentation multiple times and we would have a flood of prospects approaching afterward. As a result our customer acquisition costs were extremely low for an enterprise software product. Customer funders can be an incredibly valuable market maker, and once we figured it out we became very strategic about leveraging.

Getting back to the elusive traction, who do you think also values customers being funders of a company? That's right investors. There is no better validation of a company than financially engaged customers. One of the best ways to ensure investor interest is to have financially engaged customers. I've had the chance to see a lot of pitch decks and investor pitches and not surprisingly the startups with the best traction lead with it and the ones that don't have it, don't. In fact the startups that don't have paying customers or very few, focus on everything but that and inevitably the investors get around to asking about customers, revenue, and profit. Let's put it this way: financial engagement from customers is undeniable, including for investors. Venture investing is all about risk mitigation. Investors are looking for significant upside, with less risky bets. Customer funding checks both boxes.

A relatively new venture firm understands the value of customers as investors and has created a model where the Limited Partners (LP's) in the firm's fund also become early customers of a startup they are investing in. The firm is Heartland Ventures and I love their model. Customers as investors and investors as customers is brilliant. I would expect more venture firms and funds to adopt this model.

Funding through customers, even if you end up taking non-customer investment, is still the best way to fund the company. Funding through operating revenue and profit is always preferred, with customers as investors a close second.

## CHAPTER 28
# Culture and branding

There is a lot of conversation and content about culture these days. What is culture? How do you create it? How do you make it good? There is an endless stream of culture opinions, recommendations, and advice. We've hit peak culture from a chatter perspective, but in many cases not successfully from an execution perspective.

One thing on which I do agree with most of the "culture" chatter is the importance, especially for a startup. Every company has a culture. It's just a matter of whether it is intentional or allowed to happen without regard to what kind of culture is manifesting and taking root. For startups, the culture emanates from and is a direct reflection of the Founders, the moment the company is started. This is one of the reasons Founder self-awareness is so important. How do the Founders make decisions? How do the Founders deal with problems? How ego centric and driven are the Founders? All aspects of how the Founders act informs and creates the initial culture of a company. And the initial culture of a company is very hard to overcome if it isn't positive, productive, and reassuring. The culture of a startup is directly related to how you start and ultimately determines where you end up. I really like the metaphor of how you start determines how you finish across many aspects of life and business. Start a product the wrong way and getting back on track is exponentially harder. Start a company the wrong way and ditto. How a company starts from a culture perspective likely determines the company's culture for the duration of the company's existence.

I've always looked at culture as not something a company has, but what a company is. The best definitions and explanations of what culture is are centered around the sum of the decisions and actions (both macro and micro) that the company makes naturally day in and day out. My interpretation of this is when people in the company are making unconscious decisions and just acting, what is intuitively driving those decisions and actions? What fundamental beliefs and principles are at play beneath the decisions and actions that are driving them? This is culture.

At AWH, the product and data consulting firm, where I am a Partner, we have established core values that we operate on as our foundation that are centered around two guiding principles:

1) Work in the best interest of the product/problem and

2) Work in the best interest of the client.

These principles and the values on top of them drive our culture.

A startup, yes, even yours, has a culture. It is based on how the team makes decisions and takes action. You might have a cool space, a snazzy logo, and a dope site but these things aren't your culture. They are representative of your culture, but are not your culture. The thought process and decisions to pick the space, to go with the logo, and to make the dope site is your culture. The individual items are expressions of your culture but not the culture fabric itself.

Founders and the team's decisions and actions are what the establish and define the culture. So if you are to be intentional about your culture, be intentional and aware of how you make decisions, what actions you take, and how you take those actions. If you want a decisive, fast moving culture, be decisive and move fast. If you want a methodical, well-planned culture, decide and act that way. Where Founders and startup teams can often feel and be stressed is when they are acting incongruently with their culture. Saying your culture is one thing, but acting incongruently and inconsistently will cause undue stress and pressure on the team and company. To be in alignment with and to be living the culture you have, you must pay more attention to actions than rhetoric. The rhetoric is what you think you are supposed to be saying, but the actions reveal who you really are. Having a misaligned culture will create unnecessary negative team dynamics and decrease overall performance, which often results in team turnover. A startup with a lot of team turnover that is capitalized well enough for whatever stage it is in is almost certainly experiencing a culture challenge.

Two areas that are difficult to change downstream for a company are culture and branding. These are also two areas that are consistently under-valued and under-appreciated by many startups. A company's brand is a reflection of its culture. Not the other way around. I see many startups attempting to define their culture by their branding and when they don't connect, they don't know why. I'm not a culture or branding expert, but it seems to me that branding should be an outward expression to a great degree of a company's culture. Many companies try to have the branding in front of the culture because branding is at least slightly more tangible and definable. A brand is manufactured and produced, while a culture is an amalgamation of all of the decisions and actions of the company. But neither can be taken for granted and allowed to develop on their own. An out of control and unintentional culture and brand becomes hard to wrangle, and when you want to become intentional about them, they will push back with all of the legacy baggage that is now embedded in them.

A word of caution around branding, though. As I've seen many startups not be intentional about branding, I've also seen a number of startups out-brand their ability to deliver on what their branding would indicate. This is a delicate balance for startups, especially early stage ones, as early stage startups almost always have to appear bigger, more capable, and more consequential than is the reality of their current state. Establishing a strong brand is important and a requirement for every startup, but having the brand be authentic to who and where the company is, is also important. Don't out-brand too far beyond what the company can and will deliver on in the relatively near future.

# Product Flow

## CHAPTER 29
# Introduction

Creating anything great is incredibly hard. Creating a successful product is no different.

Defining what a successful product is seems like a good place to start. My definition of a successful product is one that solves a high-value problem that customers care enough about to pay for, at a level that provides the business outcomes desired by the product owner. There have been a lot of products over time that met one side of the product success definition, but not both. Those are not successful products, because they are not sustainable. For a product to be successful, over time, it needs to provide value to the customer and the owner.

Freemium became all the rage during the 2000s as a product pricing and go-to-market strategy. It actually became so popular that it evolved from just being a pricing/customer-acquisition strategy to becoming a business model and product approach. For the most part, freemium did not live up to the promise of helping products and companies to be successful because it focused almost entirely on the customer and not enough on the business needs of the product owner. Turns out it is really hard to convert a non-paying customer to a paying customer if the value proposition between the free version and the pay version isn't significant. Customers stay with the free version and the product owner (company) has an unsustainable product and company as a result.

Some of the components of achieving Product Flow in this section are:

- Get and stay close your customers. How to do it and why we don't. I refer to this as the "One thing" Jack Parlance principle from the movie *City Slickers*.
- Why you need to understand the problem at an expert level and how to do it.
- Understanding that ego is your enemy and how to overcome it.
- Complexity bias is real and why simple and elegant is possible in any circumstance.
- Seeking negative but honest feedback during validation will give you the real insights you need.
- Why customers focus on what isn't in the product.

What I cover in this section will help anyone creating a product. Whether you are an entrepreneur creating a product and a new company on top of it, part of a corporate team creating new products, or anything in between, you can use this book to help you navigate the process and increase your odds of success by achieving Product Flow. Product Flow not only helps to ensure product commercial success but it also helps you get there faster and less expensively.

*Note*: Wherever "Customer" is used you can insert "User." I use "Customer" as the universal reference for anyone using a product. I prefer Customer because it reinforces my definition of a successful product.

CHAPTER 30

# Roadmap
# (and an Agile rant)

Roadmaps are under fire. The debate around the value of roadmaps has never been more intense. People on both sides make somewhat compelling arguments. The debate exists and people call into question the value of roadmaps not because roadmaps aren't valuable, but because people devalue them.

Roadmaps have too often deteriorated to be nothing more than features against a production timeline. As a result the roadmaps have little to no value. A superficial list of features across a timeline was never the intended value and use of roadmaps. We've reduced them to be inconsequential. Roadmaps are not to blame. We are, as product people.

To make roadmaps produce the value they can provide, product teams need to use them in a deep and meaningful way. This means context and narratives around the features that are deep and meaningful. And when I say deep and meaningful context, I mean way beyond what you are probably thinking and doing. I know a unicorn startup (valued at over a billion dollars) that has pages of context and deep narratives around every feature and potential features in their products. They value the deep context and narrative even more than they value other things such as standup and scrum that other companies put a lot of focus into. By the way, they are right. The deep product context and narrative reduce the need for Agile tenants that become crutches for many product teams and companies. Being great at roadmaps makes the other activities less important or at least less likely to become crutches. I'm not a huge Agile fan. I get a lot of pushback whenever I bring up my views on the value of Agile. Agile in its purity is fine. Problem is Agile gets bastardized and then it loses its value. I also think it becomes a crutch that then prevents companies from becoming great at product. Great product teams don't need Agile. A lot of Agile consulting firms and consultants have made a lot of money on the back of Agile being the savior for companies. Shame on them. They know that for the most part they are selling an elixir and not dealing with the core issues. The consulting firms and consultants don't deserve all the blame though. Technology executives do, too. Agile became the latest and greatest elixir so they jumped onboard, instead of dealing with and getting better at the fundamentals of being great at product. Hundreds of millions, probably billions, has been spent on failed and misguided Agile implementations and transformations. This can only be categorized as professional malpractice by technology executives and leaders. If you've adopted Agile and you aren't any better at building valuable and successful products, be honest with yourself, stop focusing on agile and start focusing on the things that truly matter like deep feature context and narratives.

**Agile methodology** is a type of project management process, mainly used for software development, where demands and solutions evolve through the collaborative effort of self-organizing and cross-functional teams and their customers."

So, yes, I believe you should have a roadmap for your product. Roadmaps are not good or bad unto themselves and using them correctly provides significant value. With that said, what matters more and what you and I should care about more is the feature/functionality context and narrative. If you are creating deep context and narratives, then you may be able to build a successful product without a roadmap in the truest sense of what a roadmap is. But if you are creating the context and narratives and then prioritizing based on value and impact, guess what, you have a roadmap. Prioritized feature/functionality based on great understanding and insights is a roadmap.

**CHAPTER 31**

# Hypothesis

The best product people and teams are constantly forming and working to prove or disprove a hypothesis. In fact, the process of creating and evolving a product is a series of hypotheses being formed and proven or disproven.

Forming a good hypothesis is relatively straightforward in concept, but hard to do in practice. A good hypothesis is well thought out and well articulated. Yes, even the wording of a hypothesis matters greatly. The best product teams spend a lot of time and energy establishing and nailing their hypotheses. Well-crafted and meaningful hypotheses also drive well-crafted and meaningful user stories, job stories, and functional requirements. The best product roadmaps begin with the best hypotheses.

Great hypotheses aren't wrong or right. They are precise and free of ambiguity. Proving a hypotheses right is not the objective. Proving it wrong can be just as valuable. The outcome of a hypothesis and the creation of a new hypothesis is what makes the process valuable. The redirection is the value. We're not wired to view hypotheses this way though. The truth is we are biased as soon as we create a hypothesis. By the very act of creating the hypothesis we are intending for it to be correct so we can be correct. This is why it is always important to have hypotheses reviewed by others and to not create them and act against them in a vacuum. Left on our own we will strive to prove hypotheses correct even in the face of dissenting evidence and proof. I like nothing more than to see a hypothesis trail and evolution around a product. The longer the trail and the more evolution that takes place means the product team is open to being wrong, yet resilient in the pursuit of the right answer.

Hypothesis execution drives humility among product teams. As a product team keeps evolving and redirecting from hypothesis to hypothesis the team has to remain egoless. The desire to be right gets replaced with the search for the truth and accuracy. Once a product team gets to this point the team is performing at an elite level, likely in all areas of the product.

Hypothesis execution is an important piece of overall product execution. It's the tip of the spear. If you want to be great at product, get great around hypotheses.

CHAPTER 32

# Feature Seeking

I was meeting with one of our clients at AWH recently and she made an observation that everyone creating a product for the first time goes through: customers focus on what's not in a product, rather than what is. This is especially true in early versions of a product. It's one reason we don't ship as early and often as we should.

For first-time product builders this is a surprising and disheartening experience. A lot goes into even the smallest, simplest of products and it can be challenging when customers, who in some cases have even helped define that initial functional footprint, almost immediately disregard it and start asking where the rest of it is. Customers aren't intentionally trying to be difficult. Turns out there is science behind this and customers are doing what all of us are instinctively wired to do.

Neuroscientist Jaak Panksepp's book, *Affective Neuroscience*, describes how seeking is the most important of the seven core instincts of the human brain. The others are anger, fear, panic-grief, maternal care, pleasure/lust, and play. As it relates to early products, customers are seeking. Their seeking for it to do more, because even the actual process of seeking for the product to do more provides unconscious feedback that makes us feel good when we focus on what isn't there versus what is.

Nevertheless dealing with what appears as customer negativity at best and disingenuous at worst is hard for product creators. Here are some tips to position and soften the blow:

Before showing a customer the product, preface the interaction in writing and verbally what is included and what is excluded. Referencing what is excluded will diminish the customer's innate desire to seek.

In the excluded list it is best to provide a roadmap and anticipated timeline for the additional functionality. If you don't take this additional step, customers will still be in seeking mode asking when the excluded items will be added and in what priority.

Be prepared to discuss and defend the roadmap prioritization and timing, but only to demonstrate the thought that has gone into it. Also express and be willing to take feedback on the roadmap, otherwise you might seem inflexible or tone deaf to early customers. And of course you should also have a degree of flexibility to ensure the roadmap and product align with what customers value and will pay for.

Product creator's ability to navigate customer seeking well will go a long way in getting early product buy-in and adoption. Customers that get and stay in seeking mode too long can actually lose their enthusiasm and interest in a product. I've experienced this and witnessed it many times. Customers who seek for a product to do and be more eventually fatigue, and you would think that means they just become happy with what the product does. This isn't the case. Customers who are left in seeking mode too long actually end up becoming disinterested in the product because the seeking becomes uninteresting and unfulfilling. This is why the exclusions and roadmap from above are so important. It helps to prevent customers from getting "seeking" fatigue—customers won't express their seeking desires somewhere else, because they're seeking being satisfied with you.

**CHAPTER 33**

# Speed Matters

You're probably not moving fast enough. When we think we are moving fast enough, we're not. You should be moving uncomfortably fast when creating new products.

When I say you should be moving fast, I'm not necessarily referring to how fast you map out UX flows, design screens, or write code. You should be producing work fast as a given. I'm referring more to decision making, learning, and redirecting.

I see too many product teams getting paralyzed by decisions and then moving too slowly. The best product teams know they will never have all of the information they need to make decisions, but they have a sense of urgency to decide based on the information they do have and they act. You are not creating a product in a vacuum. Your customer's businesses are changing. The market is changing. Competition is changing. The longer it takes for you to make a decision the more change has occurred and that increases the likelihood you are going to make the wrong decision or already have by not making any decision.

Product teams are becoming obsessed with quantitative data and analytics. While this isn't an inherently bad thing, the quantitive has to be combined with qualitative customer feedback and your vision/roadmap for the product. Remember, a successful product provides value for the customer and the product owner. Quantitative usage data also means you have enough customers using the product for the quantitative usage data to have value. When you are early in the product creation process, you will have no usage data or very little. You will have to make decisions combining your conversations with customers and potential customers, the little usage data you might have, and your vision for the product.

You should be paying attention to usage data from the outset. The first version of the product, the first customer uses, should have analytics built in. You need to know from the first customer, how they are using the product and how that aligns with what customers said they would do and how you envisioned the future of the product experience.

Our team at AWH was engaged with an enterprise to help them assess and validate some new products with an underserved part of the market. During the engagement, customers were asked during in-person sessions what potential product concepts they liked the best and they were asked to rank five concepts.

A product doesn't care who is creating and owns it. But it does care about the process of how it gets created. Assuming you have skilled, committed team members creating the product, the product expects the team to be decisive and to progress quickly.

Moving quickly also engenders confidence in the team, customers, investors, and partners. Your ability to evolve and enhance the product consistently demonstrates discipline, expertise, and commitment that does not go unnoticed by all key stakeholders.

Releasing product updates frequently helps you learn faster and to correct missteps sooner rather than have the missteps lingering for a long period of time. Technical debt, as it is often referred to, is a situation where a product continues to get updated on top of prior missteps in architecture, technology stack, code, or all. The longer the technical debt exists the more painful, more complex, and more expensive it is to correct. Evolving the product frequently actually reduces the amount of technical debt because you can correct the missteps sooner as you constantly update the product. When a product languishes between updates, it is more difficult to take care of the technical debt because the focus is on the new features and functionality. This is counter-intuitive, but I have experienced it myself and seen it across hundreds of products now. Moving fast helps you learn faster and correct more previous missteps than moving slowly does.

CHAPTER 34

# Get and Stay Close to Customers

I'm consistently surprised how product teams either don't get close or stay close to users. Most product people are aware of the Lean Startup, the Agile development methodology, and other iterative approaches to create new products. Yet, many product people and teams can't wait to get as far away from users as possible. I believe they know they are making a fatalistic mistake, but they don't care. They don't care because they would rather create a bad, unsuccessful product than interact with users throughout the process to build a valuable, successful one. So if most product people know they should iterate closely with users, yet they don't, why? It's ego and fear. If you haven't read, Ryan Halladay's book, *Ego is the Enemy,* I highly recommend it. It's astonishing how much of an impact our ego plays in preventing us from conducting ourselves the way we would like to and accomplishing our ultimate goals. This ego paradox is counter-intuitive and ego is the primary reason we don't get and stay closer to users while building products.

## Value learning over knowing
My colleague and friend Dan Manges, Co-Founder and

CTO, ROOT Insurance (also former Co-Founder and CTO at Braintree, acquired by PayPal) said to me once that people and organizations need to switch from valuing what we know to learning. This is a massive shift in thinking. Enterprise companies especially pay people for what they know, not their ability to keep learning. Valuing what we know over learning is a significant Achilles heel when creating new products. It causes us to solve and create in a vacuum and then to unveil new, uninteresting, low-value products to users who might not have asked for them and probably don't want them.

You might be a visionary and be able to see what customers need before they do, but you increase your odds of success with the product if you get and stay close to customers through the entire lifecycle of the product. If you don't get and stay close to customers throughout, you risk getting out of alignment with them and creating something they don't value and won't pay for. Remember, this is about increasing the odds of success, not feeding your ego and not playing hero.

One reason large corporations aren't as good at creating new, successful products is that large corporations don't get and stay close to customers. In fact, larger corporations have created a program to represent their customers instead of having customers at the table, iterating with them on the product. These customer representation programs at large corporations are most frequently called Voice of Customer or VOC. Yuck. Forming a program to represent your customers instead of actually engaging with them continually through the product creation process is a cop-out and lazy. It's also one of the primary reasons large corporations suck at creating new, successful products.

This is not to say that startups get this right most of the time either. They don't. I've seen far too many startups that do very little customer engagement and if they do it at the outset, they quickly migrate away from it. You know, because customers are inconvenient and engaging with them is messy and complicated. Of course it is. Humans are messy and complicated. They will tell you they want one thing when they really want something else. They have emotions and an ego that skew their judgment and give us misinformation. However, if you don't dig in with customers and stay dug in with them your chances of creating a product they value and will pay for is virtually zero.

Getting and staying close to customers forces us to be disciplined through the product creation process. This is crucial because most people are undisciplined. When I am speaking at conferences on product, one of the ways I demonstrate to the audience that most people are undisciplined is through health and fitness. As mentioned in *Chapter 4: Discipline,* I ask the audience if they agree the two fundamental principles to being relatively fit and healthy are 1) To eat relatively well and 2) To get consistent, strenuous exercise. This is outside of any disease or physical ailment that affects someone's fundamental physical wellness. Everyone in the audience agrees these are the two principles and then I ask how many people in attendance are as fit and healthy as they want to be given they acknowledge there are only two principles and achievable by anyone in normal health. Consistently only 1 to 2 percent of the audience indicates they are as fit and healthy as they want to be. So 98 to 99 percent of people at product conferences at least acknowledge they are undisciplined.

The discipline of getting and staying close to customers forces us to be scientific through the product creation process and less sporadic in our mindset and approach. Creating a product requires us to overcome several human flaws to improve the odds of creating a product customers will value and pay for. The more grounded we stay in a well-defined process, the odds of us creating a successful product increase in direct proportion to the discipline. The product creation process is truly a scientific endeavor. We have a hypothesis and we set out to validate or invalidate our hypothesis. The only accurate and meaningful way to validate or invalidate the hypothesis is by getting and staying close to customers through the entire process.

Airbnb is now recognized as a standard bearer for being a great product company. From delivering a simple and elegant user experience, to a user interface that is clean and clear, they consistently get it right. They've really gotten the product right from the earliest days because they got and have stayed close to their customers. Co-Founder and CEO, Brian Chesky said this, "We would go door to door in NYC, or Denver where the DNC was, literally meeting with, staying with and living with our users." Every product team creating a new product should be in sleeping bags next to their customers on the floor just as Airbnb did.

The magic of developing the discipline of getting and staying close to customers is that it becomes part of your DNA and culture. If you can cross this threshold into valuing customer input to this level you will eventually find a way to solve a problem they value and will pay for. I firmly believe that an average person or product team who spends enough time with customers through a disciplined process will eventually solve a high-value problem the customers will pay for.

So how many customers should you get and stay close to? This will vary over time as you have more customers using the product, but I wouldn't get too crazy trying to iterate intimately with too many customers as long as the customers you are iterating intimately with are deeply committed and engaged. Ten seems to be the magic number at any given time. It gives you enough people to have a diversity of perspective without being unmanageable.

## CHAPTER 35
# Outcomes Over Outputs

The best product people value outcomes over outputs. The challenge isn't producing work. The challenge is producing the right work at the right time that produces the outcomes customers and you mutually value.

Driving to outcomes over outputs is harder to achieve than it initially appears. Driving to outcomes means we first have to establish what problem we are solving with our work to know whether we are accomplishing the desired outcome. After defining and understanding the problem, we have to define the desired outcome, or at least an acceptable outcome. Once we've established problem and outcome alignment, then we can begin to work on the problem and drive to the outcome.

We get caught up in outputs because we're wired to produce. Production feels like progress. Production feels good until we realize we produced the wrong thing, not enough, or more than we needed to. All of which are wasteful at best and maybe fatalistic for the product at worst. Product teams should not be measured or judged on the amount of work they produce. They should be judged and measured on the quality of the outcomes from the work they produced. This is a very different perspective and the best product teams understand this principle and don't waver in their execution around it.

The best product teams are iterating on the product

continually and producing high-value work consistently that drives valuable outcomes for the customers and themselves. So don't mistake being outcome focused for not iterating often and swiftly on the product. Being outcome focused actually allows you to get more work done, faster and for it to be the right work versus work for work's sake. Being outcome focused assures you are using your time, team, and energy to the optimum level because you are only doing work that is centered on the most important outcomes, right now.

The outcomes you are driving for now will most certainly change over time as your customer problems change and evolve, as the product matures, and as your business on top of the product evolves. Outcomes are a moment in time. You will always be iterating with customers on the product to solve new problems or legacy problems in new and different ways to drive new outcomes.

One of the ways to ensure you are valuing outcomes over outputs is to establish a clear and concise measure for an outcome. If you get x result from customers using this functionality you have produced the desired outcome and if you don't get that usage result, you haven't and you keep iterating until you do. Let's take an example of customer-onboarding to the product. A new customer signs up to use the product in whatever mechanisms you've provided for them and they begin to interact with the product in a haphazard way and then never login again. Onboarding new customers to a product is very common problem and one that every product team needs to figure out for their product. You could begin to work on a bunch of different things to try to affect the problem and output a bunch of work hoping that something works and sticks.

## CHAPTER 36
# Ship Early and Often

Most of us involved in creating products have now heard or seen the quote from Reid Hoffman, "If you aren't embarrassed by the first version of your product, you shipped too late." Many people don't take the time to understand why he said it and why it matters.

The first challenge with shipping products early and often is ego. What Reid's quote doesn't say, is why we don't ship early, even if we know we should. Our ego is what prevents us from shipping a product early. Knowing the product isn't what it could be and some day will be, makes us defensive because we take people's negative opinions about the product personally. And our perspective is understandable. Creating anything is a very personal endeavor. Software is no different than creating a new painting, sculpture, building, or song. The creators are inside of the creation. It's impossible to separate the creators from the creation. The difference between software products and most other things, is software can be released and evolved quickly and often, where other things can't be. This iteration and evolution difference challenges our egos and demands we release something we know has shortcomings to learn more from customers actually using it for the long-term benefit of all.

The second challenge with shipping products early and

often is we believe, and sometimes it is true, that we will only get one shot. Customers are demanding and have a lot of choices. One of the choices customers have is to do nothing. In fact, this is the choice of most customers. They simply won't see enough value in how you are solving the problem to want to take action on it, to use your product, or to keep using your product. It is a tall order to provide enough value in your first product that customers believe you have crossed a value proposition threshold that makes sense for them to use the product irrespective of the product's shortcomings. This is why understanding the problem at an expert level and always driving to the simplest most elegant way to solve the problem is critical. These two principles help you overcome your fear of shipping early, while satisfying the customer's value need.

## CHAPTER 37
# Small, Committed, Skilled Team

Beyond getting and staying close to customers and deep problem understanding, the team is the next most important aspect of product creation.

The best product teams are a small, multi-disciplinary team of highly skilled craftspeople. This is fairly harsh analogy, but think about a team of Navy Seals. All team members are highly trained and highly capable. The whole team understands the mission, the vision, the problem to be solved, the principles the team will operate on, and what outcome(s) solving will produce for all stakeholders. As with a product team, a Seal Team's members know every other team member's role and how they fit into the overall mission, even though the team members have their own domain expertise.

A Seal Team is likely to have someone who is responsible for communications, someone else who is an explosives expert, someone else who is a navigator, and so on. Product teams should have an engineer (maybe two or three depending on the technical scope of the problem being solved and what front-end and back-end development is required), an IX/UX (Information-Data Experience and User Experience) architect, a UI (User Interface)/brand/visual designer, and a

Product Manager. Sometimes it also makes sense for product teams to have QA (Quality Assurance), DevOps (Development Operations), and a Project Manager depending on where the product is in its evolution. The QA, DevOps, and Project Management team members can probably be fractional across several product teams.

Experience has proven product teams of larger than five dedicated team members begin to complicate the work and the team becomes less efficient and productive. The reason this happens is because context and collaboration are paramount in creating successful products. Context and collaboration are too often under-valued and as the product team expands beyond five, maintaining the context and required level of collaboration becomes more challenging. This is especially true considering that product teams should be iterating and redirecting quickly with customers as they become more informed and find better, simpler ways to solve the problem.

Context and collaboration seem easy to achieve. They aren't. Even among a small, committed, and skilled product team misalignment and misunderstanding occurs easily and often. Product teams should check in with each other and customers in a marginally uncomfortable frequency. When a Seal Team is executing a mission, they stay in constant communication because any single team member not having the context every other team member has and being on the same page around how the context is affecting the mission is a recipe for disaster. The same is true for product teams. Creating a product is an exercise in progress, not an exercise in perfection. Proper progress is dependent on each team member executing in alignment with the other teams at all times.

When a Seal Team is executing a mission there is no designated leader throughout the entirety of the mission. Seal Team members switch who is leading constantly and dynamically during a mission. The dynamic leadership approach allows for the team member who is most confident and capable at a point in the mission to lead for the best interest of the mission and the team as a whole. Egos get set aside and the team follows whoever is leading, based on what the situation calls for. The same should be true for product teams. At some points development should lead. At other points design or product management. It is no single team member's responsibility to lead, nor should it be. Given the fluid nature of creating a product and the constant new discoveries that are happening, leadership needs to shift as needed to best serve the product and the team.

When trying to accomplish anything of consequence and with immense obstacles the smallest, most-collaborative, best-prepared teams, win. Mt. Everest climbing teams are small, typically not more than ten people. Seal Teams are a small operating group as referenced above. If you want to build a new, innovative product, assemble the most highly skilled, committed, and small team you can. Not one more person than you absolutely need to be able to operate with speed, precision, and fluidity.

## CHAPTER 38
# Don't Find a Solution Too Early

One of the challenges we have as an end-to-end product creation firm at AWH is clients wanting to know what we're going to create even during the pre-engagement conversations. We see it in RFP after RFP. "Submit an initial design, workflow, and user experience" as part of your response, the RFP states. Clients in early discussions about the product will also ask if we can give them a sense of what it will do and look like, even in the first meeting. Prospective clients ask us to show what we will do because they're wired to create, as we all are, and because judging designs and user experiences gives them some tangible things to compare firms with. I get it and doing this has major flaws and negative consequences for anyone creating new products.

We're all wired to build. It feels like progress. It feels like real work. It produces tangible outputs. And before we have deep problem understanding, it is wrong. Finding a solution and building too early means we are building the product in our own image of what it should be based on our limited knowledge of the problem. In the end, we're guessing. This is why creating user experiences before having enough context is bad, even though it makes us feel good. Building products is a delicate balance of moving uncomfortably fast, while doing so properly with patience.

Finding a solution and building too early also has a way of surviving even in the face of direct customer feedback and validation with a dissenting perspective. Early designs, workflows, and features end up in the product because we want them in there. We created them. It becomes personal, when it shouldn't. Doing this forces customers to denigrate what we've done but most won't, so it survives and we take it as confirmation we are right, when we're not.

I was in a meeting with a Fortune 500 company about a new product they were considering creating to serve a particular set of customers better. The meeting was for them to give me more context about what they were thinking, for me to offer advice, and potentially for us to engage as a firm. As they started describing the situation, one of the team members said he knew just what to do. He declared the solution was, "A dashboard." He seemed very convinced. I asked him how many customers he had validated this with and how. He said none, but that he didn't need to because he had been at the company for 27 years. He said his experience told him the solution was a dashboard. At the risk of coming off like a pretentious jerk, I politely told him, which means I started my remarks with, "With all due respect," that's always a telltale sign that what is to follow is not that pleasant. I told him he was finding a solution too early and since he had done no validation with customers his experience was actually more likely to be wrong than right. He responded with, "We always build dashboards for these kinds of things." I asked how that had worked out for them. Everyone else immediately jumped in with, "Not well." He also then admitted they did not have a great track record of creating new, successful products that customers valued and used. You see, this guy probably does know a lot about the industry and how the company works and he couldn't help himself in thinking of the solution too early. Most of us can't. It's how we're innately wired and that's one of the reasons creating successful, valuable products is hard.

When you catch yourself finding a solution and building too early and/or building beyond what you've validated with customers, here are some things you can do: Ask, "Has this been validated with customers?" "How much of it?" "When?" "What did we learn?" "How have we incorporated or otherwise what have we done with the customer input?" Question the solution until it can be defended or not and then figure out where to go back to.

If you are going to increase your odds of creating a successful product you need to fight the urge to find a solution and build too early. If you do find yourself on occasion solving and building too early, and you will because we all do, pause to question everything about it and be prepared to throw it all away and restart. There is no harm in throwing it away and restarting. Better to do that than to move forward with something that is just wrong with no chance of success.

## CHAPTER 38
# Pay Little (no) Attention to Competitors

I often get push back on this opinion but I feel strongly about it based on my experience. When building a new product, I would recommend paying little, really no, attention to competitive products. If you pay too close attention to competitive products while building a new product, there are conscious and unconscious negative ramifications that far outweigh the benefits.

### Lack of problem understanding
Paying too much attention to other products informs our view of the problem through how the other products are attempting to solve it. The risk here is that the other products may not be solving the problem in a high-value way that customers value and in fact should this be the case you probably shouldn't be pursuing a product that does. The other products are likely not solving the problem because the product team probably didn't have deep problem understanding. If you knowingly or unknowingly take some cues from other products on how to solve the problem and you don't invest the time to understand the problem at an expert level yourself, then you and your product have no advantage over the other products.

## Me too product

Spending too much time, energy, and attention on competitive products typically means your product will end up doing many of the same things, in the same way as the other products. You can't unsee what another product does and how it does it, even as much as you say you are just using the other product understanding for competitive intelligence. Seeing and using competitive products when we are creating a new product early on taints our perspective and every aspect of our product. There is no point in building a me-too product. Customers won't value it, investors won't fund it, and people won't find it interesting enough to work on.

## Customer centricity

We already know most products are not created iteratively enough with customer feedback and input. Paying too close attention to competitive products causes us not to get enough customer feedback and input. It's easy to get sucked into the trap of seeing other products and even unconsciously starting to create our product in the image of the others with some subtle changes that in our minds seem to be tremendous differences. When we let other products drive our product's roadmap, we have acquiesced control to the other product teams and we have also drifted away from customers. And given that the other products likely lack customer centricity and problem understanding, following in the other product's footsteps is a fundamentally flawed approach.

## Competitor success or lack thereof

Even if a competitor or more than one is succeeding or

appears to be on the surface, you don't know the true state of the product and company. Don't assume that because they are getting a lot of buzz that all is well. Buzz is often temporary and of course can now be purchased and manufactured without much substance behind it. If you have chosen to create a product to solve a problem you care about, then the thing that matters more than anyone else's success is your ability to solve the problem in a way that customers value and will pay for. Don't get caught up in a competitive product's success. Focus on what is within your control and succeed based on your own ability to drive value for customers.

## Product approach

I see a lot of product teams mirroring the ways other product teams have created a product. This is across the spectrum of methodologies, systems, tools, technical stack, and code. I was speaking with someone recently who said they were going to build their product in a particular language because that's what Facebook uses. When I asked them what other technical approaches and languages they considered, they said none, "If it worked for Facebook, why wouldn't it work for us?" It's not all bad to look at clearly successful products to understand the underpinnings, but you also have to be responsible to build your product with the best approach for it, not someone else's product.

We provide technology due diligence services at AWH where investors considering making an investment in a software company engage with us to review the product architecture, technical stack, and code. When we ask the product team/ Founders how they made the technical and code decisions they have, they frequently say one of two things: 1) We used the programming language we know best or 2) We did what XYZ did for their product. These are both risky approaches. Forcing a programming language and technical approach onto a product that doesn't support what the product is and needs to do is a failed approach. All product technical approaches and decisions should be grounded in doing what is in the best interest of the product, irrespective of what anyone else has done with a different product.

## Outwork and outperform

Paying too close attention to competitors saps Founders of time and energy that could otherwise be used to outwork and outperform them. In virtually every scenario in life when you are paying too much attention to what someone else is doing, you are giving them power and control over your time and energy. Time and energy are irreplaceable. I would say they are even more important to Founders, given the pace and intensity that building a product and starting a company requires. Founders can't outwork and outperform their competitors if they invest any more time than necessary in understanding a competitor's strategy and model. Founders need to learn what they need to about competitors at a high-level and then get back to work.

I would encourage you to ignore competitive products, especially while you are in the early stages of creating yours. If you have validated you are working on a problem that customers care about and you are iterating closely and frequently with customers, nothing a competitor does matters.

## CHAPTER 40
# Don't be the X of Y

Don't be the Uber of this or the Airbnb of that. I see a lot of pitch decks and pitches where a product gets positioned as the X of Y:
    X = existing well known product
    Y = the space for the new product.
This is a cop-out and lazy.

We want to do the X of Y reference for people so they can more easily understand the application and use of our product. This is mostly a result of bad advice from the elevator pitch era I now hope we are exiting. Elevator pitches never provided much value and never really changed the trajectory of a conversation with an important stakeholder like a customer, team member, partner, or investor. Anyone that has ever said give me your elevator pitch is not that interested in what you are doing, They are using the elevator pitch time as a way to stall to come up with their disinterested response or they are looking for reasons to have a disinterested response, based on what you say or don't say during the pitch. Referencing your product as the X of Y will lose credibility with stakeholders, especially investors. The practicality is investors have heard countless X of Y pitches, and although they were part of the problem helping the X of Y refrain to occur, investors know companies using the X of Y crutch almost never materialize into anything of substance. The X of Y crutch highlights a lack of depth and understanding of the problem and customers. If you understand the problem at an expert level and are iterating closely with customers you don't need the X of Y crutch. Nothing screams naiveté more than saying you are the X of Y.

The mindset of being the X of Y is dangerous for the product owner because it draws an irrelevant comparison of product states. The X being referenced is that product at a now evolved and mature state, not what the product was early on. I speak with a lot of early product owners who references X's and say that's what I want version 1 of my non-existent product to be like. I then show them the early versions of X and say this is what you really are talking about since the X being referenced has evolved over 10 years and has millions, if not hundreds of millions of dollars, behind it to date. The typical reaction is a gasp of how bad the early versions of X were, but still a denial that the new product can't look like the X ten-year product versus the X early product. Then the therapy session starts.

It's also dangerous to take the way another, even successful product, works and apply it to your problem and product. But this is what happens when we start thinking and positioning our product as the X of Y. We start, many times unconsciously, to actually make our product work like and look like the X we've been referencing and holding in such high regard. The way a ride-share app works may have nothing relevant to the way your product should work to solve the problem you are working on. I was speaking with a Founder recently who is trying to make the transition from prototype to version 1 of the product. She referenced Uber and said she wants to be the Uber of her space. I pointed out the differences in the problems being solved and the services being offered between her company and Uber. She dug in her heels and started protecting her position of being the Uber of Y. She was protective and defensive because she had told herself and others so many times that she was going to be the Uber of Y now she needed to defend that position versus being focused on the problem, her understanding of the problem, and her unique approach to the problem. Being the X of Y has lasting, negative consequences that can't even be seen on the surface.

Recruiting, marketing, sales, product management—everything seems to be easier with an X of Y reference. As with investors, we believe everyone will get what we're doing, why we're doing it, and how we're doing it easier and faster if an X of Y reference is used. Until the reference starts to fall apart as in the above Uber example. And then we lose credibility. Don't be lazy and don't use X of Y references for your product. If you've been doing it stop, immediately. Put the time and thought into how to have your product story stand on its own. If you can't get there, then evaluate whether you should be working on it and pursuing it at all. A product story that needs an X of Y crutch is a story that doesn't end well.

## CHAPTER 41

# The Best, Not First, Product Wins

It used to be that being first was everything. It was hard to unseat the first entrants into a space because the first mover advantages were significant. Being first came with a moniker of respect. This company, this product was the first to identify the problem and do something about it. Being first mattered so much that often the best products didn't win, the first ones did, even if they weren't as good as the follow-on products. There are exceptions of course, but being first created competitive moats and snagged market share even when the product didn't warrant it. Bad products got rewarded and lauded just because they were first. This meant that sound product management and a good product discipline often didn't exist even in companies that were regarded as innovative and successful. Because bringing products to market was expensive, time consuming, and laborious, being first meant an unsurmountable advantage in many cases. Product build cycles were longer too. Everything took longer and was more expensive. Times have changed.

It has never been easier to build products and to make them available. However, just because it is easier to build and distribute new products, it doesn't mean it's easier to build *great* products. In some ways the ease of building and distributing has made it harder to create great products. The ease of creating and distributing causes us to create shortcuts. Shortcuts to maybe be first, but shortcuts that don't result in the best. The build part can happen and building a product well is still vital, but the problem and customer understanding is the most crucial part. It always has been and will always be. When it took longer to build products, this part could be diminished in importance because being first also meant buying time to figure things out better. New products always need more time to bake, but there is a big difference between releasing a product to be first than releasing it to be valuable from the outset.

The ideal scenario is to be first and best. But if you can't be both, be best. The best products win now. If you understand the problem at an expert level, stay close to customers, and build something they value, you can get a lot of other things wrong and still have the opportunity to succeed. If you don't, you won't. You can't market, sell, spend money, PR, or anything else your way to success now. The product has to be great. Anything less than a great product gets treated as such by customers. Being great at product is the new competitive moat and it isn't optional. Without a focus on building the best product, everything else is irrelevant. Even if you aren't first, you will be moving so fast on your product that the time between being first and where you are won't matter much.

What does best mean? Every product is a work in progress with no finish line, just different points in time of the product's evolution, so best is relative to a degree as every product may not have yet achieved its best state. I look at it through the lens of the problem and customer. The best products at every stage are the ones that honor the essence of the problem and reflect it in the product. Doing this creates value for customers at every stage too. The best products are magnificent in their simplicity and provide significant value to customers because the product team understands the problem deeply. The best products are a manifestation of a product team's problem understanding and their ability to reflect it in a product. Best rarely means biggest and fanciest. Usually it is the simplest and most elegant. Simple and elegant comes from deep problem and customer understanding. Best means the product does precisely what it needs to at every stage and nothing more. And the product accomplishes it in a manner that is easy to explain, understand, and use. The best products are as close to zero-friction for customers as possible. The pursuit of Customer Product Fit has become so important and you hear so much about it now because we now know being first doesn't matter as much as being the best.

Since you won't be paying undue attention to competitors and you won't care about being first, you can focus your time and energy on the problem, customers, and building the best product.

# Final Thought

I was asked by a participant in i.c.stars|*COLUMBUS what my definition of success is. I didn't have a great immediate answer so I told them I would think about and get back to them. Over the following weeks I tossed around and analyzed lots of ideas and aspects of how success could be defined. I thought about it in the context as a person and our profession/work. I thought about it as a Founder, creating products, and startups. I ultimately landed on this: success is the fulfillment of potential. A person's individual, unique potential. A product's potential. A company's potential. The fulfillment of potential is all we can really ask for. The opportunity to fulfill potential as a person, product, and company is unique and special. Every person has a different set of talents, skills, hopes, desires, and goals. The fulfillment of potential is the maximization of all that someone or something is and can be. I conclude with this challenge for you. Focus on fulfilling your potential as a Founder, for your product, and your company. Don't worry about and focus on nebulous success. If you fulfill potential you are successful, whatever your personal, product, and company potential is.

# Acknowledgments

My Partners at AWH for the support during our time together as business partners in the firm over the past 8 years (the firm has been around for 25 years and they are two of the three original Partners) and during the writing of this book.

Our team at AWH who show up every day to ply their craft on behalf of our clients to build great, successful products that improve people's lives and drive the outcomes desired by our clients. The AWH team operates under two guiding principles that I believe all professional services should. First, we work in the best interest of our clients. Sometimes this means challenging conversations as we collaborate and guide them through the process of building software products and solving data problems. In many of our engagements, our clients are building their first or at least their first major software product, and solving data problems that are negatively impacting their organization's ability to serve their stakeholders. Because we are operating from a more informed position than our clients about the process to build software products and to solve data problems, we have an absolute obligation to honor the more informed position and to engage with clients in a responsible manner. Second, we work in the best interest of the product and problem. We have no agenda and don't force-feed technical approaches, programming languages, or tools that aren't in the best interest of the product and problem. We have several tools and platforms we are certified partners for and their owners often get frustrated with us because we won't just blindly sell their platform or tool. We're committed to working in the best interest of the product and problem not a platform or tool vendor.

We are privileged to have amazing clients at AWH. We have clients working to improve communities, businesses, and people's lives everyday. And I mean truly improving lives. From a mental wellness and suicide prevention client, to an organization that has raised over $200 million for cancer research, to a digital healthcare platform that provides physical wellness capability for everyone, irrespective of physical limitation, to one of the nation's leading community philanthropic organizations that is changing what it means to be a community foundation through great digital platforms. We have clients across virtually every industry and across the spectrum of startups, mid-market, non-profits, and the enterprise. The AWH team and I are humbled by your trust and privileged to work with you. You can learn more about some of our work and clients at www.awh.net.

Startup Grind is a global community for entrepreneurs (www.startupgrind.com) I have had the great privilege to be a part of for the past seven years. Our values are:

*Give more than you take.*

*Make friends not contacts.*

*Helping others before helping yourself.*

Our global Startup Grind family educates, inspires, and connects more than two million entrepreneurs across 600+ cities. I don't use family loosely in the Startup Grind context. I have met some incredible people, who have become some of my closest friends, through Startup Grind. If you are an entrepreneur or have thought about starting a company, check out your local chapter, attend the global conference, or start a chapter if there isn't one in your city yet. There is always more room in our global family.

I became acquainted with a program, i.c.stars, in Chicago several years ago and fell in love with the people, their work, and their impact. The program (www.icstars.org) trains under-employed adults to be technologists and leaders. After becoming aware of the program I decided to launch the first expansion location outside of Chicago in Columbus. The impact we've had in Columbus is outstanding and we're just getting started. Thank you to i.c.stars|*CHICAGO for paving the way and 20 years of commitment to provide awareness and access to under-estimated people. I will be eternally grateful to the Columbus people and organizations that have dug in and supported our work. The best is yet to come.

I needed to find my own Flow to write this book. I ended up discovering that I was the most productive writing at coffee shops, first thing in the morning. I also realized I did my best, most productive writing near the busiest area of coffee shops, near the ordering counter. The constant flow of traffic and conversations around orders helped me focus and created just enough noise to force me to be and stay focused on what I was writing. So I became a Columbus coffee shop vagabond. I've overstayed my welcome at coffee shops across the city.

I always purchased something. Thankfully I love everything about coffee and coffee shops. I've come to appreciate coffee shops and the role they play in our communities and lives even more. Columbus has a thriving and outstanding coffee shop scene. Thank you for providing an environment that helped me accomplish this book and enduring the time I spent in your establishments.

I also discovered I can produce high-quality work and perform at a high-level for about 90 minutes at a time. Whenever I tried to push much past the 90 minutes my level of focus and quality of work suffered. This probably isn't an epiphany and has been the case for a long time; I just never internalized and understood it to the level I do now. This is also probably true for most people. It's one of the reasons that creating something is often a long and arduous process. I've known this as part of creating software products and now I know it as part of writing a book. I've read where authors have said it took them several years to write a book. I used to scoff at that, thinking how hard can it be? Just sit down and write. I now understand and appreciate the process. As with any craft, you can't continually crank out great work. The great work comes out in between periods of reflection and re-energizing.

I've been fortunate to have many organizations, events, and conferences engage with me to speak about building products, innovation, and starting companies. Thank you to all who have had me speak. If you are part of organizing an event or conference and would like to discuss me speaking, please send me a message at speak@ryanfrederick.co.

# About the Author

**Ryan Frederick** is a Founder and product person at heart. Ryan has had the privilege of being part of starting and growing several software and service companies. He has helped companies grow from inception, to viability, through to sustainability. During the evolution of these companies, Ryan has served on company boards and been instrumental in capitalization activities. He has also helped companies expand to international markets. Ryan combines a unique blend of business acumen and technical knowledge, having originally been a developer who migrated to the business side. He now helps companies build great software products and solve data challenges for competitive advantage as a Principal at the product and data consulting firm, AWH. Ryan, an active angel investor, mentors and advises entrepreneurs and start-ups, as well as corporate innovation leaders. He launched a non-profit workforce development program, called i.c.stars, to train under-employed adults on digital skills. In addition to authoring this book, Ryan speaks frequently about the product, Founder, and startup journeys.